EAST EUROPE IN SEARCH OF SECURITY

EAST EUROPE IN
SEARCH OF SECURITY

By

PETER BENDER

Translated by

S. Z. YOUNG

THE JOHNS HOPKINS UNIVERSITY PRESS
Baltimore, Maryland 21218

for

THE INTERNATIONAL INSTITUTE
FOR STRATEGIC STUDIES
LONDON

Published in the United States of America
by The Johns Hopkins University Press
Baltimore, Maryland 21218

Printed in the United States of America

Library of Congress Card Catalog Number
72–4313
ISBN 0–8018–1441–3 (clothbound edition)
ISBN 0–8018–1442–1 (paperbound edition)

The English edition includes certain additions
to the German edition *x Sicherheit Befürcht-
ungen in Osteuropä*, published by Kiepenheuer
Witsch Koln Berlin in 1970.

Published in Great Britain by
Chatto & Windus Ltd., London

CONTENTS

Foreword   *page* ix

WHAT DOES 'SECURITY' REALLY MEAN?
Security against What Kind of Danger?   2
Security for Whom?   7
Security against Whom?   8

THE GERMAN DEMOCRATIC REPUBLIC
I THE SPECIAL CASE   10
Outpost of the Socialist Camp   10
The Belated Ally   12

II DANGERS   14
The GDR's Enemies   14
A Danger of War?   16
Symptoms of a Military Threat   19
'Penetration'   21
Ideological Dangers from the West   23
West Berlin   26
Ideological Dangers from the East   27
The Dangers of an East–West Agreement   28

III SECURITY POLICY   29
Goals and Principles   29
(a) The Framework   29
(b) Alliance with the Soviet Union   31
(c) Consolidation of the GDR   32
(d) Unity in the Camp   33
Methods   34
(a) Military Policy   34
(b) Economic Policy   36
(c) Home Policy   37
(d) Policy on Germany   38

IV IDEAS AND PROSPECTS FOR THE FUTURE   41
Disarmament and European Security   41
Normalization of the GDR   45

v

POLAND

I LESSONS AND CONSEQUENCES OF THE WAR 48
   The German 'Drang nach Osten' 48
   The Oder-Neisse Line 51

II DANGERS 53
   Danger of War 53
   Dangers in the West 54
   Relations with West Germany 56
   Dangers from West Germany 59
   Dangers from a United Germany 62
   Relations with the Soviet Union 64
   'Rapallo' Fears 66
   Ideological Weaknesses 67
   Three Cases of Ideological Danger 69

III SECURITY POLICY AND PROSPECTS 73
   The Alliance 73
   Proposals on European Security 75
   Planning for the Future 79

CZECHOSLOVAKIA

I THE HISTORICAL BACKGROUND 82
   The Lessons of the 1930s 82
   Post-War Policy 83

II DANGERS 85
   The Danger of War and the Ideological Threat 85
   Relations with the Germans 86
   Relations with the Soviet Union 88

III SECURITY POLICY 90
   Basic Principles 90
   Security against the East 91

IV PROSPECTS 95

HUNGARY

I THE HISTORICAL BACKGROUND 100

II DANGERS 102
   Danger of War 102
   Ideological Dangers 103

III Security Policy   104
IV Prospects   107
   Hungary and Europe   107
   Regionalism   109
   Pragmatism   110

RUMANIA

I Geographical and Historical Background   112
II Dangers   113
   War, the Germans and 'Softening up'   113
   The Threat from the East   115
III Security Policy   117
   Presuppositions   117
   Internal Politics   117
   Foreign Policy   118
   (a) Loyalty and Threat   118
   (b) Theory and Practice of Bloc Policy   119
   (c) Policy Outside the Pact   120
   Results   122
IV Concepts of the Future   123

BULGARIA

I Geographical and Historical Background   125
II Dangers   127
   Dangers from the West   127
   Dangers from the East   128
   Ideological Danger   129
III Security Policy   130
   Relations with the Soviet Union   130
   Balkan Policy   132
IV Ideas of the Future   133

CONCLUSIONS

I Dangers   135
   Fears of the West   135
   Fears of the East   137
   Consequences   138
II Security Policy and Concepts of the
   Future   140

FOREWORD

A necessary prelude to agreement is understanding. People in the West, in their anxiety to protect themselves against dangers from the East, have often not given enough thought to the fact that in the East, too, people are anxious for protection against danger from the West. Both sides demand, as they always have, security. Both sides proclaim that this should be created through a 'security system' or 'peaceful order' for the whole of Europe. Not much in this direction has been done so far. But if more is to be done, it seems necessary to have a clearer idea of the fears and wishes of the other side.

The purpose of this book is to make a contribution to this end. It is limited to the security concerns and policy of the six states today linked to the Soviet Union in the Warsaw Pact. The Soviet Union itself is not dealt with—Moscow's security problems are no longer a European question, but a global one. The Kremlin's special relationship to the United States of America, the other nuclear great power, seems to be more important for its security than its relations with Western Europe. The confrontation between NATO and the Warsaw Pact is only part—an important part—of the opposition between Washington and Moscow, between East and West. On top of this the Soviet Union is having ever greater difficulties with China.

The states between the Baltic and the Black Sea, which are discussed here, lie in the ideological and power-political field of tension between the Soviet Union and the Western alliance. To establish what their security concerns are, it is first necessary to examine the real meaning of 'security' in their position. Is it merely protection against military dangers, or is it something more? Secondly, it is necessary to consider the special circumstances of each individual country—not in order to elaborate contradictions, but so as to take natural differences into account. Since there is much that is the same, or similar, the first two states considered, the GDR and Poland, have been treated more fully than the other countries. Otherwise there would be too great a risk of repetition. The second and more important reason for the varying length of chapters is the fact that the security problems of individual countries also vary in extent. The main purpose of this book is to look at the European scene through East European eyes. It is their opinions, not those of the author, that have to be set out. And since one cannot write a whole book in indirect speech, some of what appears without qualification is only, or mainly, the view of others.

Basic sources are of three kinds:

1. Official statements from political speeches to press articles.
2. The general literature on these countries. In order to keep down

the number of references, these are given only when an assertion rests especially and exclusively on a particular source.

3. Personal knowledge obtained mainly, though not solely, during visits to the countries dealt with. Where no source is given, a statement or assertion quoted comes from a private conversation.

The English edition includes certain additions to the German version, which was completed in early summer 1970. The treaties of Moscow and Warsaw, intended by the Federal Republic to establish normal relations with the Soviet Union and Poland, have changed the image and standing of West Germany in Eastern Europe. The English text has taken account of these changes, so far as limitations of time allowed.

I owe to the International Institute for Strategic Studies in London, where I was able to work for a year (during which the *Westdeutsche Rundfunk* most generously allowed me leave), both the stimulus and the opportunity for this project. The Institute provided me with contacts and made it possible for me to undertake two journeys without which I could have done no more than recast one set of printed sources into another. I feel especially indebted to the former Director of the Institute, Alastair Buchan, and his successor, François Duchêne, for their interest and their help. I wish to thank my friends Carola Stern, who has taken an interest in the German edition, for her advice and criticism, and Christoph Bertram for his help, both as an Assistant Director of the Institute, and in other ways.

PETER BENDER

EAST EUROPE IN SEARCH OF SECURITY

WHAT DOES 'SECURITY' REALLY MEAN?

When five Warsaw Pact countries sent in their troops to occupy Czechoslovakia on 21 August 1968, they were convinced that they were protecting their security, and that of Czechoslovakia, against the West. When, in the preceding weeks, realists among the Czechs warned their leadership of the possibility of military intervention by their allies, their intention was to protect the security of Czechoslovakia against the East. The five occupying powers feared two things above all. On the one hand they feared a weakening of Communist power in Prague so far-reaching that Czechoslovakia would be delivered up to Western influences and the European balance of power between East and West be upset. On the other they feared that their own parties and countries might be infected by the example of the Czechoslovak reforms. Their first anxiety was directed towards the West and was, in the last analysis at any rate, a matter of international power politics. The second however was directed against an East European country and was a matter of ideology and internal politics. The danger here was not to their countries as such but to the regimes at present in power and their interpretation of Socialism. In Prague and in Bratislava the situation looked quite different. They were gaining sympathy in the West. The danger came only from the East, a danger that threatened not only the leadership but the whole country, and might appear in forms ranging from political and military pressure to surprise occupation.

This example shows the wealth and variety of points of view that have to be taken into account in any discussion of security considerations among Warsaw Pact states. In this context it has to be borne in mind from the start that in politics it is not the facts that are decisive, but beliefs about the facts. What a country and its government do about their defence is not determined by whether they are actually threatened, but by whether they feel threatened. Of course there is almost always a connection between actual and apprehended danger, and in the ideal case the two are identical. But the ideal case arises only occasionally, and even more rarely are the more irrational quantities involved. In general—as far as one *can* generalize— dangers are more likely to be over- than under-estimated. An appearance of danger to one's life inclines one to be more cautious than analytical. Dispassionate analysis of the facts becomes difficult or impossible, or is ignored in the face of strong feelings arising from historical experience—sometimes extending over centuries—from ideological prejudice, and above all from the personal background of the generation in power. In these circumstances awareness of actual dangers is repressed, while dangers that have long since faded are exaggerated. In addition there are often reasons of propaganda for ignoring the first and exaggerating the second. And if this goes on for years or even decades, the victims are not merely the consumers of this propaganda but to some extent its producers as well, who gradually, in their efforts to persuade others, become convinced themselves.

Most of these phenomena are not confined to Eastern Europe, but they are more marked there. A viable concept of security for this part of the continent must measure up to subjective standards—a security problem exists where it is felt to exist. Of course this definition is not always adequate. It is known that in the summer of 1968 hardly anyone in authority in Prague believed there was a military danger. None the less there was a danger, and this danger in fact became a reality that has dominated all considerations of security in Czechoslovakia ever since. So our definition must run as follows: a security problem exists where people are conscious of it or will become so within a foreseeable period.

But what does this mean in practice? The example of 21 August 1968 shows that three questions arise here: 1. Security against what kind of danger? 2. Security for whom? 3. Security against whom?

Security against What Kind of Danger?

Security in the ordinary sense is a question of war and peace. For a state it means a guarantee of protection against military attacks from outside. But now that the boundaries between war and peace have become fluid and national interests are mingled with ideological conflicts and affinities, this 'ordinary' concept of security is often inadequate. In Western Europe this is much less true today than during the 1950s when fear of 'Communist subversion' still played an important role. But in Eastern Europe, so far as it belongs to the Soviet system of alliances, 'security' still means more than protection against NATO's tanks and missiles. It is true that the word itself is almost always used to refer to military conflict—often in the UN Charter's phrase 'peace and security'. None the less one can only build up a complete picture of the security requirements of individual East European states if one takes into account a class of dangers, popularly termed 'softening up', for which a whole series of names have been invented in Eastern Europe: agitation by the class enemy, imperialist infiltration, ideological subversion and diversionary activity, peaceful counter-revolution, 'muffled' aggression. The problem here is that of internal political developments which are or seem to be bound up with foreign policy in their origins or their consequences, as can be seen from the main examples—the East German rising in 1953, the Hungarian revolution in 1956, and the Czechoslovak movement towards democracy in 1968.

Taking the consequences first, we know that the workers' demonstrations in Berlin on 16 June 1953 began with a demand for reduction of work norms, but a few hours later had already adopted the slogan 'free elections', which at that time meant reunification of East with West Germany. The revolt in Budapest also began with socio-political objectives and ended with the announcement of withdrawal from the Warsaw Pact—a withdrawal frustrated by the overthrow of the Nagy government. The five occupying powers feared a similar development in Czechoslovakia in the summer of 1968. In their Warsaw letter they wrote to the party leadership in Prague: 'We cannot . . . agree to hostile forces thrusting your country away from the Socialist road and conjuring up the danger of a separation of Czechoslovakia from the socialist commonwealth.' It is possible to make out, from a number of statements, how they thought this might happen. The Communist Party loses it leading role, i.e. control over political developments— this was the decisive charge against Dubček—and is sooner or later forced into the background or dissolved by 'counter-revolutionary' and 'anti-socialist' forces. The means of production may continue to be socialized, agriculture collectivized and educational opportunity made equal, but the country ceases to be 'socialist' in the sense that matters—in terms of political power.

Ideological changes become a danger to security when they touch on questions of power. That is equally true of foreign policy and of internal policy, especially in the minds of Communist statesmen. In their eyes a change of regime sooner or later brings with it a change in foreign policy alignments. Thus the Warsaw letter says: 'The frontiers of the Socialist world have advanced into the heart of Europe, to the Elbe and the Bohemian Forest . . . we will never allow imperialism to make a breach in the Socialist system and alter power relationships in Europe to its advantage, whether by peaceful or non-peaceful methods, from within or from without.'

'Peaceful' methods probably means here, in the first place, a mixture of economic seduction and 'revisionist' influence. Czechoslovakia was to be bought back by and to capitalism. The fear that a Socialist country might fall into economic dependence upon the West is well known. The measure of what is acceptable is political reliability. A 'safe' man like Ulbricht can allow himself more Western trade than an 'unsafe' one like Dubček.

'Non-peaceful' methods might take the form of armed uprisings incited and supported by the Americans or the West Germans. There are East European commentators, and not especially conservative ones at that, who in general do not exclude such possibilities. In explanation there are occasional references to American policy in Latin America.

But whatever methods were to be used, the decisive motive for the occupation of Czechoslovakia—so we are assured by both theorists and practical men in the occupying countries—was fear of a change in East-West power relationships in Europe. One may dispute whether developments in Czechoslovakia justified this fear. But if this were the case, there could be no doubt of the necessity for intervention. The way of thinking about security revealed here is essentially the same as that of the West. Confrontation, or at least competition, between the two blocs is so sharp that any disadvantage to one's own side inevitably becomes an advantage for the other, and this is thought to be insupportable. All reflection on security begins and ends with the balance of power. The only difference is that the Warsaw Pact takes into account much more strongly than NATO internal political disturbances. This difference is of course vitally important in practice. Efforts at reforms such as those in Czechoslovakia during 1968 would be taken much less seriously by their opponents if they did not—in fact or in appearance —operate to the benefit of 'imperialism' and thus became a danger to Socialism.

At this stage, if not before, consequences are linked to causes—and not only by conservative observers in the East. It is widely supposed that the beneficiary of an event must be the one who caused it. This is especially true of Communists who are taught to have regard above all to what is 'objective', to consider effects rather than motives. It was owing to this kind of thinking, as well as to the needs of propaganda, that each of the major mishaps of East European Socialism from 1953 to 1968, and many minor ones too, were traced back, completely or at least in part, to the activity of the 'international class enemy'. This can be illustrated by a recent example. In the autumn of 1968 an article in the Soviet periodical *International Affairs* asked what it was that made it possible in Czechoslovakia for the 'counter-revolutionaries to influence considerable sections of the population'. The answer given was as follows: Despite very extensive social changes since 1948, the bulk of the former exploiters and high officials had remained in the country and had not changed their essential class character. The same thing could be seen in other People's Democracies too. Mass emigration among anti-socialist sections of the population had occurred only from the German Democratic Republic (GDR), from Hungary after 1956, and to a certain extent from Poland.

This explanation follows Marxist lines, though in a very superficial way. The class enemy within supplies a basis for the operations of the class enemy without. Here as in all history we are dealing with a class struggle. At the same time this interpretation offers two advantages. It suggests the soothing conclusion that everything will come right as soon as the remnants of the old society have emigrated or died out. Above all, however, it makes it possible to avoid the main and painful question of how opposition arose among those who ought not to have been anti-Socialist, either by origin or upbringing—among workers, young people, and large sections of the Party.

The Communists' refusal, or inability, to recognize basic weaknesses in their own system is, however, only a partial explanation. Certainly none of the acute crises in Eastern Europe have been induced by the West (if only because the West is just as frightened of explosive developments). But it is equally certain that intellectual and therefore political processes in Eastern Europe as well are influenced by those in the West. And this is in part deliberate. Western broadcasts aimed at Eastern Europe still often contain a considerable amount of propaganda. And even when they only give information, they constitute a standing irritation to states whose internal system requires a government monopoly of information. Nevertheless there have arisen, especially since the mid-1960s, whole political strategies aimed at gradually loosening up the Eastern bloc economically, ideologically and politically, and eventually dissolving it.

To the Western observer all this does not seem very important. He knows—to take only two prominent examples—that Professor Brzezinski, who is so much feared in the East, has had little influence on the conduct of American foreign policy; and that the 'revanchiste' bogey-man, Franz-Josef Strauss (Adenauer's real successor in foreign policy), is actually not in the least interested in Eastern Europe and only clothes his plans for Western Europe in a pan-European programme because the current mood demands it (just as Adenauer did with his erstwhile pan-German programme). In Eastern Europe, however, people see first of all that Strauss is one of the most powerful politicians in the Federal Republic of Germany, that Brzezinski worked for a time in the State Department, and that the Bonn Government appears to have adopted his plans for the isolation of the GDR.

When Western statesmen talk about a 'Marshall plan for Eastern Europe', about agreements and bridge-building, this often seems, to the other side, to be simply a camouflage for new ways of fighting Socialism. It is striking how the writings of conservative authors in the East towards the end of the sixties about the efforts of NATO countries (especially America and West Germany) to promote *détente* use, very largely, expressions applied ten years earlier by the West to 'peaceful co-existence'. In each case the argument follows the same pattern: 'Thanks to our strength the other side now shrinks from direct aggression. But they have by no means given up their intentions. They are simply pursuing them with different, more subtle methods. The danger has not become less, but greater.'

The one-sidedness of this way of thinking is (and always was) obvious. On the other hand there is no denying that, in practice, a policy of agreement, of contacts and co-operation, contains risks for each party. For the Eastern side the most far-reaching, though not the only, danger is that attributed to the fact that Socialism has triumphed almost entirely in economically less developed countries, and hence has to be protected against the lure of the capitalist world. The point has been made by a commentator on the Hungarian radio:

> During the summer, when there are many foreign visitors in our country, including Westerners, while at the same time swarms of Hungarian tourists are travelling to East and West, and coming home to describe their experiences, one is struck by many things . . . Some of my countrymen, who have been in the West, come back full of exaggerated admiration, and attribute all the really interesting, new, valuable and modern things they have seen to the advantages of capitalism and the defects of their own country. They do not have the time, and do not take the trouble, to make themselves really familiar with life over there, nor do they make the effort to search for the historical or economic causes of this higher level of development . . . Provincialism has many facets. One of them is this stupid, servile admiration, without dignity or capacity for critical thought. Such admiration is always directed to outward appearances, for the man who admires never looks deeper. This characteristic arises from short-sightedness . . . Narrow nationalism fits in well with wide-eyed admiration of the capitalist world. Thus it becomes a political phenomenon not to be ignored, though one need not exaggerate its importance . . .

The slogan of 'nationalism' signifies the second ideological danger that worries many politicians in Eastern Europe, above all in the Soviet Union. What a genuine democratization means for the internal politics of a Socialist state, nationalism means for the 'internal politics' of the Socialist camp as a whole. Both weaken control, loosen solidarity, make joint action more difficult and endanger stability. The situation becomes frightening when both appear at once, as in Hungary in 1956 and, allegedly, in Czechoslovakia in 1968. Thus 'nationalism' is often considered one of the means of seduction employed by Western propaganda, and any Western policy that calls directly or indirectly for national efforts is felt as a threat wherever the unity of the bloc is seen as a precondition of security against the West.

This means that any Western effort at understanding and settlement, even if it is free of 'softening-up' objectives, becomes a potential danger. So long as East–West relations are strained, there are credible or demonstrable threats—malicious press comments, warnings or accusations from statesmen, resolutions on the strengthening of NATO. At the least there prevails a climate which encourages and enables people to make their first consideration the unity and solidarity of the Socialist countries, in both internal and foreign policy. If however relations between the two camps become more relaxed, the demands for vigilance and discipline come to seem less necessary and increasingly harder to justify. Cohesion slackens, special interests displace common interests, and national and liberal trends grow stronger. Thus for example Bonn's Eastern policy was certainly not the cause of the reform policy in Czechoslovakia, but it did smooth its path by relieving Prague, very largely, of the pressure of the supposed German danger.

The absence of danger can itself become a danger—a paradox that sometimes has very concrete consequences. *Détente* and co-operation do indeed reduce the possibility of a military conflict, but they increase the possibilities of ideological 'infection'. Thus for some politicians the question arises whether a milder, or a more harsh, policy towards the West promises greater security.

What therefore appears as an ideological danger proves to be a mixture of various elements: a mistrust born of thinking always in terms of friends and foe, the needs of propaganda, and actually existing threats, whether intended or not. Certainly the balance of the mixture is different wherever this danger appears. But the essential causes seem to be everywhere the same—an inner insecurity (for whatever reason), and a striving towards national independence. Both phenomena play a part in the problem of—Security for and against whom?

Security for Whom?

'I swear . . . to defend Socialism against all enemies'—so runs the military oath of the GDR's national *Volksarmee* (People's Army), while the five occupying powers wrote in their Warsaw letter of 1968: 'We shall never agree that these historic achievements of Socialism . . . be endangered.' So what has to be defended—and this is clear from many other documents too—is not only the inviolability and independence of the country in question, but also 'socialism'. What 'Socialism' is, is in general decided by the party leadership of the individual countries, within certain limits laid down by the CPSU. A student of East European politics has described the result, as far as present-day defence requirements are concerned, in the good Marxist statement that 'Security is always the security of the ruling group'.

This statement leads on to the connection between a state's internal and its external security. This relationship has a special importance for the allies of the Soviet Union. The less support there is for a Communist Party and its kind of Socialism among the population, the more the leadership will look to Moscow for support, and scent danger in the West. On the other hand, the more a regime has consolidated itself and its brand of Socialism—no matter by what means —the more uninhibitedly it can look to the West and the more independently it can act in the East. Thus it depends upon internal conditions whether and how far there is a difference between the security of a country and that of its regime, and whether its concept of defence is determined predominantly by ideological or by national considerations.

But regimes can change, they can become more stable or less so. Furthermore, within the next ten years a new generation will come into leading positions in Eastern Europe (in so far as it has not already done so, as in Rumania) and will influence thinking about security. A concept of security acceptable at the present time must be assessed or, better, objectively defined, in relation to two factors: How far does it harmonize with national needs? And what prospect of survival (which does not exclude reforms) has the present regime and its version of Socialism?

Security against Whom?

The threat from the West has been spelt out a thousand times— West German 'revanchism' and American 'imperialism', or a combination of the two. There are occasional and much more subdued references to the risks inherent in the confrontation of two military blocks. Nothing whatever is said of the dangers that might come from within the Warsaw Pact area itself. Officially there are none, and whether one can speak meaningfully of security questions within the Eastern bloc is a matter for argument.

In Stalin's time one certainly could not do so. After 1948–49 there was no security question in relation to Moscow for any country or any regime from Poland to Bulgaria, since all were almost totally exposed to Soviet intervention, and thus all security was almost completely done away with. The question of security had to be answered in such negative terms that it could not even be sensibly put. Since then, however, national and ideological emancipation, if to a varying extent, have made possible the development of an independence, a self-awareness, and here and there a degree of autonomy that may lead to the possibility of forcible intervention by Moscow, and consequently to reflections on their security by Moscow's allies. The increased importance of the national factor also obliges one to consider whether national causes of dispute between individual states within the Pact— as for example the dispute between Hungary and Rumania over Transylvania—might one day again reach the level of security problems. Ideological differentiation contains dangers in both directions. The more conservatively orientated regimes fear, in addition to the disruptive influence of the West, the often yet more dangerous example of a liberally governed Socialist neighbour. Conversely, the neighbour is concerned lest he become the victim of this fear.

In all this one must bear in mind the close connections that still exist between the Socialist states and undoubtedly influence their idea of security. So there may be supposed to exist among the leading groups, or most of them at any rate, a feeling of solidarity resting on the perception or fear that the fall of one could endanger the position of the others. And even apart from this, for many Communists, among the older generation at least, the 'Socialist community' still has a high sentimental value. For states and peoples the similarity in ideology, in forms of organization, and in their low degree of industrial development, creates considerable common features and also some advantages. In relation to the Soviet Union, the view exists, and is spreading (though not everywhere), that today small countries are scarcely able to exist alone and must accommodate themselves to the great powers, because they need their economic support, and to an extent their military protection. That there should be this accommodation to *the* great power into whose sphere of influence they have come through World War II and the Yalta agreements is felt, for the most part, to be an unalterable fact. None of the states that today belong to the Soviet system of alliances ever had any alternative. As a Polish scholar says, 'What is in question is not dependence as such, but only its extent.'

Nevertheless the special relationship to the Soviet Union, no matter whether from conviction, interest or force of habit, exists and as a result many things are customary in relation to Russia and seem to be advocated, that would not be tolerated in relations with Western countries. When does the inevitable accommodation become unacceptable restriction and finally intolerable injury or even a mortal threat? This in practice is a political decision. In general it can be said (and even this only with some reservation) that the question of security arises at a later stage in regard to the East than to the West. Still—whatever may be called for by proletarian internationalism and the Warsaw Pact—an indisputable limit is reached with the danger or fear of military intervention.

THE GERMAN
DEMOCRATIC REPUBLIC

The problem of European security . . . comes down
essentially . . . to the need to frustrate the West
German imperialists' policy of revenge and expansion, and their striving for hegemony in Western
Europe.   WALTER ULBRICHT

I. THE SPECIAL CASE

Outpost of the Socialist Camp

The GDR is and feels itself to be the 'Western outpost of the Socialist
camp.'[1] Of all the Warsaw Pact states it has the longest frontier with
NATO, a frontier almost without natural barriers, lying in the centre
of Europe where the armed might of the two military alliances is more
powerfully and densely concentrated than anywhere else in the world.
East Germany's northern flank consists of the Baltic coast, which in
case of conflict would be the scene of operations by the naval forces
of both sides. There is no conceivable military clash between NATO
and the Warsaw Pact, from the conventional level up to strategic
nuclear war, that would not hit the GDR at once, and probably
harder than the other East European states.

The GDR is still more of an 'outpost of the Socialist camp' in
political terms. All the Eastern countries have been, and still are,
impressed and influenced by the living standards and freedoms of the
West, especially if they border upon it. But for the East Germans 'the
West' is their own country. Events there, whether attractive, interesting, or irritating, are not just events somewhere in Europe, but in
the lives of brothers, sisters, parents, uncles and cousins. Up to
August 1961 and the building of the Berlin wall the East Germans
could compare conditions on the two sides with their own eyes, and
great numbers of them did so. Since then they have been kept *au
courant* by visiting relatives from the Federal Republic, and above all
by television and radio.

The great problem for the East German Communists has always
been to overcome this special westward inclination of their own

[1] *100 Fragen, 100 Antworten zur Wehrpflicht*, Deutscher Militärverlag,
Berlin, 3rd ed. 1967, p. 27. Cf. Brezhnev's toast, *Neues Deutschland*, 8 August
1969.

population. The Socialist Unity Party (SED) have a harder time of it than all their European brother parties. They are ruling over the smaller part of Germany (with scarcely a third of the Federal Republic's population), and the poorer (the main industrial area lies in the West). They did not get Marshall Aid, but had to pay the Soviet Union reparations for the whole of Germany. Their production and foreign trade programmes were, and in part still are, determined by Soviet interests, not their own. Even if the East German economy were not considerably impeded by ideological requirements and at times even forced down from Central European to Soviet levels, it would still have no prospect of competing with West Germany. The same applies to domestic and cultural policy. The East German leadership is neither willing nor able to keep up with the freedoms of West German democracy. Even where, over the last decade, they have been able to create institutions in the fields of health and education that are of interest to the Federal Republic also, the advantages gained in principle are spoilt by ideology or, frequently, marred by financial stringency.

The inability of the GDR to satisfy its citizens' aspirations to well-being and freedom to the same extent as the Federal Republic is bound up with the regime's main problem—the 'national question'. As a state forming part of the German nation, the existence of which the SED has continued to recognize, up to the present at any rate, the GDR can only base its existence and need to defend itself on ideological grounds:

> In the German Democratic Republic, in which imperialism and militarism have been overcome once and for all, in which the exploitation of the working people has been abolished forever, are incorporated the democratic, humanist, peaceful and Socialist traditions of the German people . . . here is the home of everything in German history that is good, fine and progressive . . . In the West German Federal Republic there prevail once again contempt for human beings, exploitation, clerical obscurantism, greed for money and conquest, and militarism. In other words, in the West German Federal Republic, under the camouflage of a seeming democracy, there is preserved and kept alive everything in German history that is backward, barbaric and inhuman, stupid and cramped, against our people and other peoples as well.

It follows from all this 'that the Socialist German state embodied the future of the entire nation, and the national question can only be solved by the victory of peace and Socialism in the whole of Germany'.[2]

---

[2] The 'National Document', *Zeitschrift fur Geschichtswissenschaft*, (1962). Text in *Neues Deutschland*, 27 March 1962, pp. 758–86.

The GDR can only survive as a Socialist state. Not to have seen this was the mistake of those—for the most part somewhat naïve—Western planners who sought to solve the German problem by turning the GDR into another Austria, a democratic state, but forbidden to merge with the Federal Republic. The East German Communist leaders, and especially Ulbricht, have always known that their state would lose the justification for its existence if it sacrificed its ideological basis. In its German policy the GDR could only choose between keeping the GDR as a Socialist state, and the reunion of Germany as a Socialist state. Since there seemed to be almost no prospect of the second, the SED leadership concentrated all their efforts on the first, not least by turning to the Soviet Union for international security.

Moscow was able to withdraw from an occupied zone like that in Austria without difficulties. To turn over a state, like the GDR, for reunion with the rest of the nation was still possible so long as it was defined in some such vague and largely arbitrary terms as 'antifascist and democratic'. But to liquidate a state recognized as Socialist and accepted into the Socialist community is something the principal Socialist power cannot do, for the same reason, among others, that the United States could not leave an unquestionably democratic ally in the lurch without losing its position as the leading power in the West. The history of the GDR's security problem is the story of two processes—construction and development of a Socialist state, and gradual inclusion in the East European system of alliances as an equal partner.

The Belated Ally

The GDR was only founded (in the autumn of 1949) when all the other countries in the Soviet sphere of influence were already 'people's democracies' striving towards Socialism. In East Germany, where the constitution was only 'democratic', not that of a 'people's democracy' the building of Socialism was not proclaimed until the summer of 1952. Next year came the heavy setback of the uprising of 17 June, and conflicts at the top of the Party which four years later still largely turned on the question of whether and how far the special Socialist development of the GDR should be carried forward without regard to relations with the Federal Republic and to the unity of Germany. Walter Ulbricht, by luck and skill, won through both times with the idea that the 'national question' must be looked at exclusively from the 'class standpoint'. 'The German Democratic Republic cannot and will not make its development dependent upon the backward social order in West Germany, when we in the GDR are already a whole historical epoch ahead of it.'[3]

[3] National Document, *op. cit.*

By the end of the 1940s all the other East European countries were already linked and bound to the Soviet Union and to each other by pacts of assistance, but the GDR remained without any treaty protection until the middle of the 1950s. Its existence was guaranteed solely by the presence of Soviet troops. This was more than enough protection against an, in any case, improbable military attack by the West. Politically however it was quite inadequate. Furthermore up to the beginning of 1955 the Soviet Union itself repeatedly brought into question the continued existence of the East German state, by proposing reunification through free elections on condition that the West agreed to neutralization of a reunified Germany. In the Federal Republic, it is true, the sincerity of these offers to liquidate the GDR was often doubted. But this did not alter the fact that from 1952 to 1955 Soviet notes and proposals greatly impeded the consolidation of the GDR and kept its wafer-thin ruling crust in constant uncertainty. They were prepared at that time, as young SED cadres were later heard to say, to carry on the struggle for Socialism in opposition.[4]

There was no treaty protection for the GDR until the Federal Republic was admitted to NATO in the spring of 1955. In May of that year East Berlin was one of the founder members of the Warsaw Pact, but only after the failure of the Geneva summit and Foreign Ministers' conferences were its armed forces officially proclaimed a national People's Army, in January 1956, and incorporated into the Eastern Alliance. The Defence Act (*Verteidigungsgesetz*—the legal basis for all non-military defence matters including regulations for a state of emergency) and the introduction of general military service did not come until 1961 and 1962, *after* the GDR Government, by building the Berlin wall, had gained the same unrestricted power over its population as the other Socialist governments.

The decisive political turning point was in 1955. In September the Soviet Union opened diplomatic relations with the Federal Republic, and a few days later regularized its relations with the GDR through a treaty 'on the basis of equality, mutual respect for sovereignty and non-intervention in internal affairs'. From then on Soviet policy on Germany was based on recognition of two German states and the ticklish problem of reunification was placed within the competence of the East German Government, in form at least. The GDR seemed to be politically secure.

But even then two things were still missing—complete equality with the other states of the bloc, and full solidarity on their part.[5] The legal framework serves as an indication of the political reality.

[4] Cf. also Walter Osten, *Die Aussenpolitik der DDR*, Opladen 1969, pp. 14–17.
[5] Thus the well-known Soviet statement of principles of 30 October 1956 speaks of Soviet troops in Hungary, Rumania and Poland, and then goes

When there were overriding interests involved, the Soviet Union has been prepared, to the end of the 1960s at least, to agree to procedures which, while they did not discriminate against East Berlin, still obviously had their origin in regard for discriminatory reservations by the West. Only in 1964 did the GDR achieve a treaty of friendship and assistance with Moscow. Only in 1967, under the influence of Bonn's new Eastern policy, did it attain full and formal inclusion in the bloc through treaties of friendship and assistance with the other members of the Pact (except Rumania). Only then did East Berlin achieve what for Bonn was a matter of course on entering NATO—solidarity with its allies on the issue of recognition. As a counterpart to the Hallstein doctrine the GDR set up, with Soviet and Polish help, the Ulbricht doctrine, a kind of unwritten obligation that each Warsaw Pact state would only open diplomatic relations with the Federal Republic after the latter had recognized the GDR as a state.

Even within its own camp the GDR only gradually won a guarantee of its existence. Its fight for equal rights with its allies was longer and probably more difficult than that of the Federal Republic. Outside the Socialist area its position is still not clear. The results of the *first* world war were accepted throughout the world. Nobody thought of questioning the existence of Poland or Czechoslovakia as states. The results of the *second* world war, however, have never been formally confirmed, they were merely accepted. For the Poles and Czechs this applies only to parts of their territory, vital though some of these are. But for the GDR its very existence is at stake. The East German state, the main area of concentration of Soviet forces in central Europe is, it is true, seen as an unalterable fact of power politics—but not as an unquestionable legal entity. Proud as the SED leaders are of all they have achieved, it is still to be assumed that this situation and their experience within their own camp, have made them specially alert to dangers of all kinds.

II. DANGERS

The GDR's Enemies

'Who is the soldier's enemy?' This is question number six in a small booklet of a hundred questions, widely distributed, on military service in the GDR.[6] The answer runs as follows: 'The deadly enemy

---

on: 'In the other countries of People's Democracy there are no Soviet military units.' Did the GDR then not count for Moscow as a People's Democracy? In any case it was excluded from the bid to negotiate over the stationing of Soviet troops. On 14 February 1958 the Polish Foreign Minister, Rapacki, in order to gain the co-operation of Bonn, suggested a procedure for negotiations on his disarmament plan that would have spared the West German Government direct contact with their opposite numbers in East Berlin.

[6] See footnote [1].

of the German nation is German imperialism and militarism which is stubbornly seeking nuclear weapons for its *Bundeswehr* and which, with the help of NATO and especially of America, is trying to carry out its openly declared programme of revenge against Socialism . . . The main thrust of West German imperialism is aimed at the GDR.'

This instruction for the troops corresponds to the documents and statements produced by the politicians. The bilateral treaties of assistance which East Berlin has concluded with the Warsaw Pact countries (except Rumania) specify as the enemy 'the forces of West German militarism and revanchism'.[7] The other Europeans, peoples and governments, so Ulbricht told the SED Party Congress in 1967, are seeking a 'system of European security' and want to preserve 'the territorial *status quo*, in the interests of peace'. Only the Federal Government in Bonn is putting 'one obstacle after another' in the way of these efforts. The conclusion of the head of the Party and state is that 'the problem of European security . . . still comes down essentially to the need to frustrate the policy of revenge and expansion of the West German imperialists and their striving for hegemony over Western Europe'.[8]

The East Berlin Government views the United States as 'the leading power of the world-wide imperialist system'. In the words of Deputy Foreign Minister Peter Florin (who supplied Ulbricht with a large part of the material for his speech to the Party Congress), the United States threatens peace in Europe because it would like, using

[7] In the treaty with the Soviet Union the word 'West German' is missing. The treaties with Hungary and Bulgaria, which lie further away geographically, contain an additional reference to 'other military and revanchist forces' with 'other aggressive intentions'. A collection of the texts of all bilateral treaties of alliance, concluded among the present members of the Warsaw Pact from 1943 up to June 1968, was published in East Berlin in 1968, entitled *Freundschaft, Zusammenarbeit, Beistand*, Dietz Verlag.

[8] This and the following quotations from Ulbricht come, unless otherwise indicated, from his speech to the 7th Party Congress of the SED, published in *Protokoll der Verhandlungen des VII Parteitages der Sozialistischen Einheitspartei Deutschlands*, 17–22 April 1967, Dietz Verlag 1967, pp. 38–81. Cf. also *Neues Deutschland*, 3 June 1969. Long passages are reproduced word for word in the corresponding sections of Peter Florin's *Zur Aussenpolitik der Souveränen Sozialistischen Deutschen Demokratischen Republik*, Dietz Verlag, Berlin 1967, which appeared shortly after the Party Congress. Thus the last quotation from Ulbricht appears twice in Florin (pp. 24 and 109)—without reference to Ulbricht. The only explanation for this coincidence is that Florin supplied material for the foreign policy section of Ulbricht's speech to the Party Congress. Later he used the same material for his book. There are interesting passages where Ulbricht's and Florin's texts in general agree, but differ in details. In these cases Florin's formulation is usually 'harder'. Thus he speaks only of the 'longing of the peoples for security, resting on guarantees' (p. 23), whereas Ulbricht assumes a 'striving by the peoples and their governments'. On page 113, however, where Florin reproduces the assessment of the Party Congress, he has Ulbricht's version, including 'governments'.

Western Europe as a 'tool', to 'hold up, indeed reverse, the historical process of the national and social liberation of peoples'. This policy was 'all the more dangerous because it rested ever more firmly upon complicity' with West Germany, which in its turn was pushing the United States into 'an even more dangerous course'.[9] In Ulbricht's view the 'West German imperialists' are intent on winning 'hegemony over Western Europe', with American help, and on carrying out their 'policy of expansion to the north, south and east'.

Thus the danger is not Western Europe, and not even NATO, but the 'Washington–Bonn axis' in which each partner is egging on the other, but the main culprits are the West German 'imperialists'. If it did not have a special enemy in the Federal Republic, the GDR would not be facing any more danger from the West than all the other Socialist states.

A Danger of War?

What does East Berlin fear from Bonn and its allies? A war? At the 1967 Party Congress the SED's First Secretary drew the following picture of the situation in Europe: The increased strength of the East—economic, political and military—was 'one of the most important reasons why United States imperialism has not yet dared to carry its aggressive actions to the point of a world war'. Dulles' plan for 'roll back', a policy of 'military force or nuclear blackmail', had proved 'impossible to carry through'. The hopelessness of the military plans of the 'American and West German imperialists' for Europe was obvious. The situation in Europe seemed to be 'to a large extent stabilized'. The peoples and most governments were striving increasingly 'to secure the *status quo* on the basis of realities, and to develop peaceful coexistence'. One could detect 'stronger tendencies towards *détente* and understanding in Europe'. In 1969, too, in Ulbricht's view, there had been no essential change: 'The European capitalist states are seeking peace and security and want to preserve the territorial *status quo*, in the interest of peace. They do not want West German hegemony over Western Europe, nor do they want West Germany to share in atomic weapons.'[10]

More important than the details of these statements, some of them influenced by the circumstances of the time, is the fact that the leader of the SED and GDR rests his judgment of the situation on the same arguments as all other European politicians. The 'growth in the forces of peace' which he takes as his starting point is none other than the East–West balance of forces, which rules out a war in the age of nuclear weapons.[11] With regard to the Federal Republic Ulbricht

[9] See footnote 8, p. 108.
[10] *Neues Deutschland*, 3 June 1969.
[11] At the 6th Party Congress in January 1963 Ulbricht declared that 'For

reckons on three factors which are not seriously disputed in the West. All members of NATO would refuse to allow Bonn a finger on the 'nuclear trigger', if it wanted one. The West Europeans view with concern the growing strength of West Germany. And they have no interest in a reunification of Germany, or its extension to the East.

Ulbricht's conclusion is that in this situation even the Bonn Government is bound to decide 'that direct action against the GDR is a suicidal enterprise'. And he goes on to deduce that the West German 'imperialists', since by themselves they are too weak, will first try to win time and to counter the threat of being isolated in the West. For this purpose they might even be ready 'to mark time for a while in their revenge policy'. Really, however, their problem is how to find an indirect way to their goal, i.e. how to create a power base from which a policy of expansion will again be possible. This programme has been supplied by Franz-Josef Strauss: 1. West German hegemony over Western Europe; 2. Securing the 'Washington–Bonn axis'; 3. 'Intrusion' into the Socialist countries, during which 'the GDR is of course to be taken over by Bonn'.[12]

This is a programme of political but not military 'aggression'. What does Ulbricht have to say about military dangers? The 'rulers' of the Federal Republic are 'aiming at new aggressions' and seeking nuclear weapons. The consequence is that 'once the West German Federal Republic controls its own nuclear warheads—this is their calculation —its aims of revenge and the whole programme of expansion can again be carried on by other means'. This, however, is only a 'calculation', and Ulbricht himself says that it runs contrary to the intentions of all the other Western states.[13] If one also takes into account that at the end of 1969 the Federal Republic signed the Nuclear Non-Proliferation Treaty, this concern on the part of East Berlin must be further qualified.

There is another significant passage in Ulbricht's speech at the 1967 Party Congress: 'The non-recognition of the GDR is intended to

---

humanity today, for relations between the presently existing states and peoples with different social systems, no other possibility exists than peaceful coexistence. War has become an inappropriate way of solving disputes of any kind. Atomic means of mass destruction and the ability to despatch them at will and at lightning speed to any point on the globe have thrown out all the old measures of military strategy.' *Protokoll des VI Parteitages der SED*, vol. 1, p. 42.

[12] Cf. Ulbricht's speech to the Conference of European Communist Parties at Karlovy Vary, where he expressed himself somewhat more sharply than at the Party Congress (*Neues Deutschland*, 27 April 1967).

On Franz-Josef Strauss's book on Europe see also the reflections of GDR Defence Minister Heinz Hoffmann, *Protokoll des VII Parteitages der Sozialistischen Einheitspartei Deutschlands*, pp. 486 ff.

[13] At Karlovy Vary (footnote [12]) Ulbricht said that the Americans stood behind Bonn's plans for expansion.

make it possible for the imperialists to represent a military intervention when it comes as, so to say, a domestic German police action, not
an international conflict, something not even bearing the character of
an act of force between states.' Ulbricht draws the same conclusion as
that which Stoph, the East German Prime Minister, emphasized to
Brandt early in 1970: Recognition is not a legal or prestige matter, but
a question of peace and European security. This reasoning gives rise
to the suspicion that the SED leadership is dramatizing the dangers in
order to back up their demand for recognition in international law.
But this is hardly the whole explanation. Apart from the recognition
question the strength of the *Bundeswehr* and its support from NATO
gives rise to vigilance and mistrust in East Berlin.

These fears, then, are not directed at improbable, foolish actions.
Ulbricht does not say, and no doubt does not believe, that Bonn
deliberately wants to unleash a world war. Hitler did not want to
either, when he attacked Poland. He hoped the British and French
would again do nothing, as they had over Czechsolovakia. Ulbricht
presumes a similar calculation in influential West German circles. He
thinks it conceivable that people might reckon there was a chance of
acting against the GDR without a world war. Hitler, and other
examples too, so they say in East Berlin, prove that 'German imperialists' sometimes miscalculate. For the generation of Stoph (1914) and
Honecker, the secretary of the Central Committee responsible for
security (1912), and Ulbricht (1893), this argument may well carry
special weight. A man who lived and suffered through the 1920s and
1930s as a Communist and knows the Federal Republic only at
second hand looks at present day West Germany from the viewpoint
of his own experience.

But there are, too, considerations and impressions drawn from the
present day. Theories of Western strategists on the possibility of
limited war meet with great scepticism in Eastern Europe. In the GDR
people are convinced that a military conflict in Central Europe would
very quickly escalate into a world-wide nuclear war. What in the
West passes for general theory, or concern for one's own security, is
seen in the East as planning for aggression. Because a nuclear war
would lay waste all parties, including the Soviet Union, Bonn is
thought to be calculating the chances of being able to occupy the
GDR by a 'police action' or *Blitzkrieg*, without massive retaliation.[14]

[14] In the *Deutsches Militärlexikon* (Deutscher Militärverlag, Berlin 1962),
the entry for 'War, limited' ('*Krieg, begrenzter*') includes the following: 'The
theory of a limited war plays a large part in the war propaganda of the most
aggressive imperialist circles, especially in the USA. In the opinion of these
circles limited war is a war conducted only with conventional weapons, combined
as appropriate with tactical nuclear weapons, with the objective of breaking
away individual Socialist countries from the Socialist camp and suppressing
the national liberation movements, in order to prepare the way for a world

The word *Blitzkrieg* has appeared in East Berlin's propaganda since the six-day war in the Middle East in 1967. It is known that the defeat of the Arabs, equipped and partly trained by the Soviet Union, came as a shock to nearly all the Soviet Union's allies. At the least it threw doubt on the dogma of Soviet superiority in weapons. For the SED this impression was strengthened by the extraordinary partisanship for Israel of the West German press and population, which thoughtful citizens of the Federal Republic felt at the time went rather too far. This was bound to disturb the other side, already mistrustful and feeling itself threatened by the Federal Republic, even if the *Bild Zeitung* had not described the armies of the GDR, Poland and Czechoslovakia as 'our Arabs'.[15] There are several examples of this kind, and their often reckless exaggeration in East Berlin's propaganda does more to conceal than reveal the genuine fears aroused.

Symptoms of a Military Threat

Even in East Berlin a West German attack is only thought to be possible in certain circumstances. The most important is certainly a strong position for Bonn within the West, something the Poles are also afraid of (p. 48). A further factor, pointed out in East Berlin in the summer of 1969, might be that the Soviet Union was too deeply involved in conflict with China to be able credibly to maintain its protective role in Europe. Thus Bonn might be given encouragement, or even real opportunity, for attacking the GDR without this 'necessarily meaning war and probably world war'. Ulbricht confined himself in public to telling the Moscow Conference of Communist Parties in 1969 that China's 'acts of military aggression' against the Soviet frontiers constituted 'direct support for the expansionist policy

war. The most aggressive military forces are trying, with the lying assertion that limited war could prevent a world war conducted with strategic nuclear weapons, to lull the watchfulness of the peoples and keep them from struggle against the imperialists' war preparations. At the present time, however, the conditions for the conduct of war have so altered that there exists the real danger that any limited war may turn into a world war. Limited wars by imperialist states against Socialist states are impossible today, since any attack on a Socialist country or several Socialist countries would be met with the armed force of the whole Socialist camp.'

Similarly an article on the principles of military thinking in the GDR expresses the opinion 'that a war in Europe would take on the character of a war with nuclear missiles from the outset or after a few days conventional fighting'. Another passage reads: 'Among West German politicians and military men voices are being raised which, in the light of Israel's aggression against the Arab countries, consider possible a lightning campaign (*blitzartiger Krieg*) limited to the use of conventional weapons, for the conquest of the GDR. This is a typical illusion of German imperialism. It would certainly prove fatal to its existence, but at the same time it is extremely dangerous to the security of Europe' (*Neues Deutschland*, 23 November 1968).

[15] *Bild-zeitung*, 14 June 1967.

of West German imperialism'.[16] If one takes account of the important part China has played in the thinking of West German politicians, from Adenauer in the early 1950s to Strauss in the late 1960s, it can be seen that these Eastern anxieties often reflect Western ideas, though in a distorted way.

More important, though never expressed, is fear lest internal disturbances in the GDR might be exploited militarily by the Federal Republic. Of course it is most improbable that another uprising like that of 17 June 1953 would occur. But this cannot be completely ruled out. Such political eruptions are of their nature unplanned, unprepared and therefore unforeseeable. They have in fact hardly ever been foreseen in Eastern Europe up to now. Those who, like the East German Communists, have experienced an uprising in their own country, will certainly not easily forget it. For the SED leadership it must be of decisive importance that today, by contrast with 1953, West Germany has a strong army. Even non-Communist observers abroad often find it hard to imagine a national army, anti-Communist by training, standing idly by while their countrymen were being shot down. A Communist, believing in the natural aggressiveness of the class enemy,[17] will consider even more likely intervention by the *Bundeswehr* in such a situation.

In the SED's view, the danger of military action by the Federal Republic would be increased if Soviet troops were withdrawn from the GDR. Improbable though this may seem for the foreseeable future, this possibility is not excluded in East Berlin for some more distant date. This is shown by, *inter alia*, a statement by Peter Florin, second man in foreign policy matters in the GDR after Foreign Minister Winzer, and his probable successor:[18]

> Any partial measure in the field of disarmament must not on any account encourage aggression by the West German *revanchists*. Thus, for example, withdrawal of all foreign troops from the two German states and removal of all foreign military bases from German soil is only possible if at the same time there is a limitation of armaments in both German states to a uniform extent and according to a unified timetable. West Germany already controls a modern, well-equipped national army which is regarded as the strongest military force in Western Europe. The GDR possesses a numerically limited national People's army which is excellently equipped and fulfils and will continue to fulfil with honour all its allotted tasks in defence of the Socialist fatherland. At the same

[16] *Neues Deutschland*, 10 June 1969.

[17] 'West German imperialism is the main focus of unrest in Europe and inevitably produces, by its strivings for power and profit, expansion, aggressiveness and danger of war.' Ulbricht at the 7th Party Congress (note 8, p. 80).

[18] *Op. cit.* (footnote 8, p. 118).

time the numerical imbalance of the two armies cannot be ignored. In face of West German militarism, armed to the teeth, the GDR needs the defence forces of friendly Socialist states, above all of the USSR.

Whatever kind of security guarantees were given to the GDR to follow a withdrawal of Soviet forces, it cannot be disputed that West German politicians and soldiers, if they wished to intervene forcibly in East Germany, would be encouraged to do so by the knowledge that they would not immediately run into Russian troops.

'Penetration'

In the East German view an indispensable precondition for military action against the GDR would be a successful 'penetration' of the Socialist countries. As Peter Florin puts it, for Europe 'the policy of "roll-back" is part of the US programme, using mainly political, ideological and economic means of diversion. The military threat from the Washington–Bonn axis remains because the object of this diversionary activity is to soften up the Socialist countries for a counter-revolutionary coup. The intention is to proceed step by step. First of all the Socialist countries are to be estranged from each other, and the GDR in particular is to be isolated.'[19]

Ulbricht took a similar line at the 1967 SED Congress. And his presumed successor in the Party leadership, Honecker, was still saying in February 1970, 'This "bridge-building" is clearly intended, as soon as the overall "climate" allows it, to enable the *Bundeswehr*, at the appropriate moment, to march across the bridge.'[20] Despite such statements, however, the military danger plays a decreasing part in the thinking of the East German leadership. Thus *Neues Deutschland* could write—at the height of the Czechoslovak crisis, on 30 July 1968:

> The European version of this global strategy at present rejects the direct use of force, since the risk is too great. Instead there is an attempt to penetrate the Socialist countries by 'peaceful' means, to disrupt them ideologically, make them economically dependent, to hollow them out from within, so that eventually, after all this well-directed preparatory work, the empty shell of Socialism may collapse almost of its own accord. Nowadays people dare not embark on a war of intervention such as was once waged against the young Soviet state. Today they are trying

---

[19] *Op. cit.*, (footnote [8], p. 56).
[20] *Neues Deutschland*, 22 February 1970.

to push back the frontiers of Socialism in Europe by means of creeping counter-revolution.

The difference from Florin's and Honecker's remarks is clear. In the one case diversionary activity is a preparation for military attack, in the other it replaces it. It is especially noteworthy that the second version comes from a definitive article in which the SED warns the Prague Party leadership against underestimating the dangers. The whole of the rest of the SED line during the Czechoslovak crisis fits in with this, both before and after 21 August, the eve of the invasion. There is only occasional mention of 'preparation for an undercover war' and of the 'plan to organize partial military conflicts'.[21] What East Berlin feared for Czechoslovakia and then for itself was a danger that was primarily not military but political and ideological.[22] Czechoslovakia was to be made into 'a centre of political and ideological diversion aimed at the whole Socialist community', into 'the centre of the policy of "rolling up" the other Socialist countries'.

The priority of the political over the military danger was also made clear in Ulbricht's speech to the Moscow conference of Communist parties in June 1969.[23] Although the theme of this conference, the struggle against 'imperialism', was calculated more than any other to depict the danger of the GDR from the Federal Republic, the East German head of state spoke much more of the economy than of strategy. For him, the 'main field' of East–West conflict was 'the struggle for the highest productivity, for the most effective form of Socialist planning, direction and organization of all social processes, the struggle for the people to live in social security, peace and happiness'. In this statement of Ulbricht's can be seen the core of a philosophy of security that applies not only to the Party leader himself and the generation of his 'grandchildren', the middle generation, but in large part also to the intermediate generation of fifty to sixty-year-olds. This philosophy is not content with the idyll of a peaceful 'competition between the systems', nor does it rule out military dangers, but these dangers are relegated to second or third place. Fear that an extra-European conflict like that in Vietnam could spread

[21] For example, 'The standpoint of the DDR', *Neues Deutschland*, 30 August 1968; 'Statement of the Central Committee and Council of Ministers on the Treaty on stationing of Soviet troops in Czechoslovakia', *Neues Deutschland*, 26 October 1968; Ulbricht the following year, at a conference of regional party delegates, *Neues Deutschland*, 3 June 1969.

[22] The following quotations, come, unless otherwise indicated, from the 9th Central Committee meeting (*Neues Deutschland*, 23 and 25 October 1968.) The conflict of the SED with the Czechoslovak reform movement is extensively documented in '*Deutschland Archiv*', *Zeitschrift für Fragen der DDR und Deutschlandpolitik* from April 1968 to January 1969.

[23] *Neues Deutschland*, 10 June 1969.

to Europe is seldom expressed in East Berlin.[24] Nor is a NATO attack on the Warsaw Pact still feared there, because the West European 'capitalists' have become war-weary after two world wars, and American nuclear power seems to be deterred by that of the Soviet Union.

Even a West German attack is seen as ruled out for the time being. The East German Communists see themselves as militarily threatened by the Federal Republic only in certain circumstances, particularly if there were to be a combination of symptoms of Eastern weakness and Western strength. The occurrence of this combination is coming to seem to them ever less probable. The real dangers to which the GDR is exposed, partly in fact and partly in supposition, are political. All the relevant and credible anxieties that have to be reckoned with in East Berlin have one feature in common—a link between home and foreign policy. Only a feeling of insecurity at home, whether justified or not, causes developments outside the GDR, which would strike a well-established regime merely as irritations, to seem dangerous.

Ideological Dangers from the West

East Germany is still especially susceptible to influences from West Germany. It is noteworthy, however, how this has decreased during the 1960s. The reasons are clear. There have been the rise in living standards, the estrangement between East and West Germans through long separation, difficulties in understanding arising from different circumstances of life, increasing resentment by the 'poor relations' against the 'rich', combined with growing pride in what they have achieved by their own efforts, and finally disappointment in Bonn's policy from which was expected in part more relaxation and in part more political aggressiveness, and in any case more credible commitment instead of fine words. All these factors eventually add up to political resignation and readiness to adapt to given, unalterable circumstances.

Of course this readiness is repeatedly disturbed. The East German Communists are Germans too, and they pursue Communism with a perfectionism and persistence that make it difficult even for well-wishers to work or come to terms with them. In addition there are the unavoidable planning failures and breakdowns which often cause trouble for the individual in his daily life, and are especially irritating in their provocative contrast to the complacent speeches about the 'superiority of the Socialist system'. All this takes on a political character as a result of the contradiction between expectations and reality. What angers people is not just the shortages of coal, or power

[24] For example Ulbricht at the Karlovy Vary Conference (Neues Deutschland, 27 April 1967); Sicherheit und friedliche Zusammenarbeit in Europa, Dokumente 1954-1967, Staatsverlag der DDR, Berlin 1968, pp. 17-18.

failures, but the fact that in 1970 the same difficulties were cropping up as in 1960, and it is doubtful whether much will have changed by 1980. Such doubts are even more strongly in evidence when there is a question of communication with West Germany, especially journeys there. Despite the general improvement in the material sphere, many East Germans lack something that Party representatives talk about most—'perspective', confidence in a permanent upward movement. There is of course little likelihood of resignation hardening into an eventual explosion. But after the disappointment aroused by 21 August 1968, in the GDR also, it can no longer be ruled out with certainty.

The SED leaders are probably judging realistically in thinking that they cannot risk increased contacts with the Federal Republic. A large part of the misunderstandings between Bonn and East Berlin, perhaps the greater part, goes back to the fact that previous West German governments have not recognized one thing, or not paid enough attention to it. This is that for the GDR an increase in links and *rapprochement* between the two German states is primarily a security problem. What in the Federal Republic are called 'humane allevia- tions' and 'softening the effects of the division' contain practical dangers for East Berlin. Every closer acquaintance with Western living standards and Western freedoms nourishes wishes and claims among the East Germans, and every relaxation in relations between the two governments arouses hopes that create pressure upon the Party and make it considerably more difficult to justify being sealed off from the West and integrated into the East. For example the pro- gramme Federal Chancellor Kiesinger offered to the Seventh SED Congress in April 1967, while indubitably for the benefit of Germans on both sides, nevertheless in political terms would have brought advantages to the Federal Republic and disadvantages to the GDR— more East Germans able to travel to West Germany, exchanges between universities and research establishments made easier, West German books, periodicals and newspapers gradually allowed into the GDR, youth groups, schools, sportsmen and cultural associations enabled to enter into unrestricted contact with each other. In the eyes of conservative East German Communists all this is nothing but laying the GDR open to systematic 'softening up' by the class enemy.

The formation in the autumn of 1969 of a West German govern- ment dominated by Social Democrats changed nothing in this outlook. On the contrary, the SED's position became more difficult. Earlier Christian Democratic Union (CDU), or CDU-led governments it could dismiss as class enemies. The conflict between the Federal Republic and the GDR could be defined as a class conflict, and the struggle against Bonn justified as a class struggle, demanding pru- dence, vigilance and reserve. This recipe is not available against a

Social Democrat government. The SED itself (the 'Socialist Unity Party') arose from a union of Social Democrats and Communists in 1946. Even the West German Social Democratic Party (SPD) is still regarded by East Berlin as to a large extent a workers' party, with which the SED hoped in 1966 to carry on a sort of pan-German Popular Front policy against the CDU. When this proved an illusion, the East German Communists withdrew from the plan already agreed for public speeches to be allowed by politicians from the SED in the Federal Republic and the SPD in the GDR.

The second reason for this retreat was fear lest Social Democratic views evoke too strong an echo in the GDR. This fear also affects East Berlin's attitude towards the Brandt Government. If there is an internal danger for the present regime in East Germany, it lies in efforts to make Socialism democratic—to do what was started in Czechoslovakia in 1968. There is fear in East Berlin that a Social Democratic government in Bonn might represent, for GDR citizens and for part of the SED, a seductive combination of welfare, democracy and socialism. It might, particularly for the other part of Germany, provide an example of how to achieve the advantages of Socialism without the disadvantages of Communist dictatorship. Accordingly Social Democracy constitutes a much greater ideological danger to the SED than CDU governments in Bonn.

Thus in December 1970 the SED leadership declared that the main threat came from 'Social Democratism'.[25] What had happened in Bonn was a change not of power but of personnel. The 'monopoly capitalists' were the real rulers of the Federal Republic, and their aim was the same as before, the subjection of Eastern Europe to West German 'imperialism'. The only difference was that the old policy was being carried on by new men, Social Democrats instead of Christian Democrats—and this was still more dangerous, since not everyone could at once recognize the wolf in sheep's clothing.

It would be wrong to regard this interpretation as simply a propaganda tactic. The image of 'right wing' SPD leaders who betray the working class and serve the capitalists, is traditional, and not only among German Communists. In addition there is a deep, almost insuperable distrust of all the forces of the West German anti-state. Twenty years after the foundation of the Federal Republic and GDR, their relations with each other are still by no means free of a civil war mentality which in East Berlin is very marked, though in Bonn it has steadily decreased since the mid-1960s. In a civil war everything is at stake and there is no compromise. In Germany today, each side would overpower the other unhesitatingly if it were able to do so. Readiness to reach an understanding has arisen only in so far as it has

[25] At the 14th Central Committee meeting (*Neues Deutschland*, 10–14 December 1970).

become clear that this possibility does not exist. The Federal Republic and the GDR only accept each other under compulsion, and since the GDR is the weaker, its leadership suffers from greater anxiety that Bonn might one day come to feel decreasing need to coexist. Just as they would and do seize every opportunity to damage the opposing government at Bonn, so they reckon on the other side doing the same. This leads to a remarkable combination of ideology and national feeling. For an East German Communist to come to terms with a French, Danish or other foreign 'class enemy' is conceivable. But it is hard for him to imagine anything more than a truce with his 'own' *German* class enemy.

Thus it comes about that the GDR leadership are much more worried about the Federal Republic than *vice versa*. East Berlin has not yet grasped that with the passage of time East Germany has become less important to the West Germans and in the policies of their government. When the SED leadership insist so obstinately on their absolute independence as a state, and want to make the division of Germany as complete as possible, the reason is that they believe more strongly in the unity of Germany and the sense of fellowship among Germans than is generally the case in the Federal Republic. For East Berlin West Germany remains the number one problem.

West Berlin

West Berlin is now only a slight source of danger. Up to 13 August 1961 its open frontier to the East constituted a weakness in the GDR that sometimes threatened to be fatal and permanently delayed its consolidation. Before the wall was built, some 2.7 million people left East Germany.[26] In the first two years afterwards, the danger of incidents leading to a wider conflict could not be completely excluded. Since then, however, West Berlin has been, for the GDR, only an irritating—indeed extremely irritating—foreign body. From the West it looks like a beleaguered island amid hostile surroundings. But to the SED it looks like an enemy bridgehead in the middle of their own territory, a centre for broadcasting hostile propaganda set up at the gates of their capital, a military strongpoint for foreign forces, with which there are no relations and cannot even be negotiations, a political base for the rival Federal Republic.

There are just two things very hard for the East German Communists to take. These are the use of West Berlin as a symbol calling in question the permanence of the GDR; and its role as a Western outpost in the ideological struggle with the East. But neither ranks as a security question, as is shown at its clearest by the reserve of the other Warsaw Pact states. The disadvantages West Berlin imposes on

[26] *Die Flucht aus der Sowjetzone und die Sperrmassnahmen des kommunistischen Regimes vom 13.8.1961 in Berlin*, p. 15.

the GDR have long since been balanced out by the advantage of being able to force Bonn, through pressure on the city and its access routes, to show a restraint it would not otherwise have to observe. The Western island in the middle of East Germany is a complication in the conflict between the Federal Republic and the GDR, but for neither side is it more than a tactical position. The decisive factor is the overall balance of forces.

Ideological Dangers from the East

The second ideological danger for the GDR consists in liberal democratic and national infections from other Socialist countries Poland first gave rise to fears of this kind. After October 1956 the GDR's relations with Warsaw deteriorated to a degree that was then unusual between Socialist countries. This only gave place to an improvement, and eventually an understanding that was at times very close, when Poland's internal policy became more conservative and both sides realized that reasons of state[27] pointed to an alliance. East Berlin's relations with Rumania became more clouded, the more resolutely Bucharest pursued its independent policy. And the SED press was the first and fiercest in its attacks on the Czechoslovak reform movement. The SED leadership showed a special interest in quelling the hotbed of unrest in Prague.

Ideological dangers from Socialist countries are perhaps taken quite as seriously in East Berlin as influences from the Federal Republic. 'Revisionism' is an even greater threat than 'capitalism'. Anything coming from the West can be attacked and suppressed as 'decadent', 'imperialist', and 'coming from the class enemy'. But developments in friendly countries carry a 'Socialist' label. They contain what is today probably the only real danger to the East Berlin regime, whether by emphasis on national peculiarities and interests, philosophical or literary theories, political reforms or simply practical relaxations. If and in so far as the SED leadership has to combat or expect serious opposition, it is from forces that wish not to abolish Socialism but to change it. If such forces came to the fore, security problems would arise anew for East Berlin, more quickly and sharply on account of the GDR's exposed position. For Moscow East Germany is the key-stone of its system of alliances. Its strategic and political interest in the GDR is exceptional, and its attitude more cautious, fearful and mistrustful than in any other case. Had a development like that of 1968 in Czechoslovakia arisen between the Elbe and Oder, we may suppose that the Soviet leaders and their orthodox adherents would have

[27] The concept of *raison d'état* is more frequently used in this connection by Poles. Ulbricht used it when he visited the Polish Party Conference in 1968 (*Neues Deutschland*, 13 November 1968).

stepped in very much earlier. In all sections of the SED, conservative and modern alike, people are conscious of this special position.

The Dangers of an East–West Agreement

East Berlin is keenly aware of the danger of external pressure from the East as much as from the West, and of eventually getting into internal political difficulties as a result. Any agreement between Bonn and the GDR's allies threatens to damage their solidarity with the SED. The more the Federal Republic succeeds in demonstrating its good will in Eastern Europe and bringing its economic strength into play, the less inclined are the countries of the Warsaw Pact to support East Berlin's hard line against West Germany. This danger is increased the more Bonn includes the GDR itself in its efforts to reach agreements and ceases to discriminate against it.

The decisive factor is, of course, the development of relations between the Federal Republic and Moscow. The SED too has its 'Rapallo' complex. From Khrushchev's time up to the signing of the Moscow treaty on 12 August 1970, there have always been signs of nervousness in East Berlin, as soon as possibilities of understanding between the Soviet Union and the Federal Republic made their appearance'. A GDR account of West German policy towards the East contains the following revealing statement: 'When West German government circles speak of their desire for "improvement" of relations between West Germany and the Soviet Union, they are always referring to some version of their revenge policy.' It is said of the former West German ambassador in Moscow, Hans Kroll, that 'He hoped that the Soviet Union would at some future date be induced to give up its alliance with the GDR.[28] This has in fact been the hope of all West German governments up to the middle of the 1960s. This hope has been without foundation since 1955 at the latest, but that does not remove the anxieties of East Berlin—because it is in the Soviet interest that these anxieties should never be allowed to die away altogether.

The signing of the Moscow treaty increased these anxieties. On the one hand the treaty does indeed confirm explicitly the inviolability of the GDR's Western frontier, and therefore provides greater security. On the other hand the very fact that Bonn and Moscow had agreed on a treaty caused intensified ideological and political insecurity in East Berlin. That Brandt, the Social Democrat, has become a trusted partner of Moscow and, since December 1970, of Warsaw too, has increased the danger of 'Social-Democratism', it has damaged the GDR's exclusive claim to be 'the German state of peace'. Still more questionable for East Berlin than Bonn's treaties with the Soviet

[28] Dr Herbert Barth, *Bonner Ostpolitik gegen Frieden und Sicherheit*, Staatsverlag der DDR, Berlin 1969, pp. 157 and 166: cf. also pp. 106 and 169.

Union and Poland is their purpose. The more the Federal Republic normalizes its relations with the GDR's two most important allies, the harder it becomes for the SED leaders to maintain the abnormal reserve in relation to the Federal Republic that they see as vital for the security of their state and regime. They are afraid of being gradually driven to defend their kind of socialism in an open 'competition between systems' with West Germany. But the GDR, in the view of most of its leaders, will lack the necessary means for this for some time to come.

The 'principal characteristic of present day international developments', Ulbricht told the Moscow Conference of Communist Parties in 1969, was 'the enormous sharpening of the class struggle between socialism and capitalism on the world scale'. The SED have stressed this idea at every opportunity for years, even independently of the Soviet Union and even in the European context, although East Berlin, too, considers that the danger of a war in that area has been decisively reduced. The solution to this seeming contradiction can only be that when the military danger disappears, the ideological grows greater. To judge from the defensive measures adopted by the SED, this is to a considerable extent what has happened to the GDR.

III. SECURITY POLICY

Goals and Principles

(a) The Framework

The external and internal policies of the GDR, more than those of any other Warsaw Pact state, are at the same time policies for security. The SED Politburo takes hardly a single decision of any substance that does not have at least a security aspect. Once the GDR succeeded, by the mid-1960s, in establishing itself as a solid, equal member of the Eastern group of states, the problem was to reach the same position in the rest of the world. The object of all East Berlin's security policy is to create as many *faits accomplis* as possible, in order to prove the finality and immutability of a Socialist German state, and to deter any attempt at liquidating or substantially changing the GDR.

This policy has its basis in the military alliance with the Soviet Union. According to the SED leaders' ideas it is only the danger of self-destruction, in the last resort at any rate, which deters the 'imperialists' of the United States and West Germany from military adventures. For German Communists the beginning and end of all security policy is the preservation of the military balance and the creation of a political balance between East and West. Second comes the effort to consolidate the East German state politically, and to strengthen it, especially economically, so as to make it less vulnerable ideologically and to increase East Berlin's political weight within the Eastern bloc. Third there is the unity and solidarity of the Socialist camp, since only this can prevent the opponent from breaking in and threatening the GDR from the flank or even from the rear. Most important is the relationship to Warsaw and Prague, which for East Berlin have something of the significance that Paris and London have for Bonn.

Eastern policy in the GDR, like Western policy in Bonn, forms the basis of all other external relations. Safety in their own area ranks before any other wish or objective. The SED leadership can hardly conceive of any gain in the West that could be worth a serious risk in the East.

This concept of security corresponds to a conservative ideology. The 'two camps' mentality of Stalin's time lives on in the SED relatively unchanged. Since war can only come from the West, the most important requirement for peace is to strengthen the East.[29] 'The conflict with imperialism has become sharper and more extensive. Thus there can be no policy of steering between the two fronts, and no "logic of the blocs". There can only be . . . a firm class position and a logic of class struggle.' Talk of a 'third way' and of convergence between Socialism and Capitalism are simply means of diversion in the 'psychological warfare of imperialism'. Even Bonn's Eastern policy seems to Ulbricht to be a 'version of the convergence theory'. In relations between Socialist states, 'national peculiarities' should only be 'understood and applied as an expression of the general underlying laws of social development'. Consequently national interests rank below the common interest, and relations with the Soviet Party are 'today more than ever the touchstone of loyalty to Marxism–Leninism and proletarian internationalism'.

An equivalent line is taken in domestic policy. The 'so-called pluralism of various parties' simply means preserving the influence of the 'class opponent'. Nor is it by any means sufficient for there to be 'the social and economic basis, national ownership of the means of production'. It is a 'fundamental error of some Socialist politicians' to believe that 'everything has been done if the problems of technical progress are mastered'. For this is to forget 'the importance of state power, the importance of the political and ideological super-structure'.

The bleak conclusion from all this is that in order to bar the way

[29] The following quotations come from Ulbricht's speeches at the 9th Central Committee plenary meeting and at the Moscow world conference (*Neues Deutschland*, 25 October 1968 and 10 June 1969), and the Central Committee resolution at the Eleventh plenary meeting (*Neues Deutschland*, 31 July 1969).

ideologically to any danger of weakness in the GDR as in the Warsaw
Pact, the SED leadership cling firmly to their largely undiscriminating
division of the world into friend and foe. And in order to be able to
take administrative action against any actual sign of weakness within
East Germany, they emphasize the 'importance of state power' with
Stalin and against Marx.

Since everything the SED leaders want to secure or introduce at
home and abroad can only be based on ideological grounds, the role
of theory has increased in the GDR as the ideological danger, from
East Berlin's point of view, has become more intense. In May 1968
Hermann Axen, candidate member of the Politburo and Secretary
of the Central Committee, ended a speech on the international
situation with these words: 'It all comes down to our intensifying
the ideological struggle against imperialism. This will enable us to
strengthen . . . our GDR on all sides and to establish it securely.'[30]
After a period of a certain laxity in the mid-sixties, intensified
ideological education and examination are again the order of the day.
But the SED wants to be active in foreign policy also. The GDR,
Ulbricht said in the late summer of 1969, was in an increasingly good
position 'to make its own proportionate contribution to the great
common cause of Socialism, peace, and security in Europe'. This
contribution did not consist only of economic and technical achievements, it related also 'to basic theoretical questions, which have to be
consistently worked through anew, in the light of continuously
developing insights'.[31]

(b) Alliance with the Soviet Union

'Firm friendship with the Soviet Union is the law of life for our people
and state,' Walter Ulbricht has said.[32] To judge by the words and
actions of the SED leadership, this law means four things above all:

1. East Berlin seeks from Moscow a permanent guarantee, the
guarantee of its existence. Thus it tries to increase the natural interest
of the Soviet Union in the East German state, through economic and
technical achievements, or through political reliability. The GDR aims
to become indispensable to the Soviet Union, and therefore inviolable
by the West. A network of long-term agreements and institutional
ties is intended to bind the GDR indissolubly to its protector.
Ulbricht is seeking in the East what Adenauer strove for in the West,
partly for the same reasons. He wants to integrate the GDR so firmly
with Eastern Europe, especially with the Soviet Union, that it will

[30] *Zu Fragen internationalen Lage und des Kräfteverhaltnisses*, Verlag Zeit im
Bild, Dresden, p. 31. The lecture was given on 15 May 1968.
[31] *Neues Deutschland*, 1 August 1969. Cf. the Central Committee resolution
of 31 July 1969.
[32] *Neues Deutschland*, 23 October 1968.

become an essential part of the Eastern system. The relationship of Russia and East Germany, which is given clear precedence,[33] is to have the same function that Adenauer envisaged for the Franco-West German relationship: to form a strong, attractive nucleus for a system that will induce or oblige others to join it.

2. Friendship with the Soviet Union is also the law of life for the SED leaders themselves. Certainty that Soviet power stands behind them is the ultimate guarantee of their regime in internal politics. The East German Communists have a greater need than any of the other ruling parties to retain credit in Moscow and to suppress anti-Soviet movements among their population before they even appear. This is the main reason for the thoroughness with which the SED, in times of crisis such as after the occupation of Czechoslovakia, floods the country with a wave of propaganda, and partly extorts expressions of sympathy for its policy. The party conducts what it calls a discussion 'on the offensive', trying to define subjects and lines of argument in advance in its own sense. This is because it cannot afford, on grounds of foreign and domestic policy alike, to be forced into a confrontation with anti-Soviet arguments coming 'from below'.

3. Close economic collaboration with Moscow does impose considerable burdens on the GDR, but it also opens up access to modern technologies that can only be developed by a super-power. This advantage, like every economic and technological advance, also means a gain in security (see also below, pp. 36–37).

4. Loyalty may pay dividends in times when it can no longer be taken for granted. The more the GDR adopts the role of junior partner of the Soviet Union, the stronger becomes its influence in Moscow, and the greater the possibility of securing help from the Soviet leaders against members of the Pact who might become a danger to the GDR on account of ideological softening or nationalistic deviation.

(c) Consolidation of the GDR

Military force is the ultimate means of defence against internal insecurity ranging from an uprising such as that of 17 June 1953 to supposed signs of dissolution such as those of 1968 in Czechoslovakia. But it is only the *ultimate* means. The SED leaders, like all politicians, want to guard against dangers before they arise. Inner stability in the GDR is the second commandment of security policy. East Germany is still a small state, so the guarantee offered by the Soviet alliance can always be improved. And the improvement here can be a substantial one, since the Soviet Union will only be ready and able to give lasting protection to a Socialist state that has established itself as such in a reasonably credible manner. Thus the security objective of all policies of consolidation is so to strengthen East Germany internally that it

[33] Cf. Ilse Spittmann, *Deutschland Archiv*, 8 (69), p. 891.

will become immune to revisionist influences from the East, and the 'imperialists' in the West will abandon as hopeless their efforts at 'diversion'.

(d) Unity in the Camp

Next to the Soviet Union no state fights so resolutely for the unity of the Socialist camp as the GDR. Unity here means uniformity in domestic policy and solidarity in foreign policy. In East Berlin it is believed that:

1. Only rigid discipline in the alliance and the same forms of regime will make it possible to hold in check national and liberal tendencies and ward off all Western threats, from military pressure through 'selective' *détente*, to ideological subversion and economic enticement.

2. The most lasting cohesion is achieved by collaboration. Ulbricht described the treaties East Berlin concluded with Warsaw and Prague in the spring of 1967, of 'friendship, mutual assistance and collaboration', as a 'defensive wall'.

> The interlocking of national economies attained or in train with the help of these treaties, their collaboration and division of labour, are speeding up and promoting the development not only of those immediately involved but of all the Socialist states. At the same time we are cutting across the efforts of the imperialist governments, above all of the USA and of West Germany too, to use their policy of 'greater movement' to manœuvre the Socialist countries into disarray and in particular to isolate the German Democratic Republic from the other Socialist countries.[34]

At the Moscow Conference Ulbricht spoke of the 'mutual dependence' that would result from economic integration between the Socialist countries.

Co-operation and division of labour are intended to restrict the allies' economic freedom of movement in relation to the West, or at least to keep it within controllable limits. At the same time they do more to strengthen the influence on its partners of the GDR—economically the second power in Eastern Europe—than *vice versa*. Besides, the integration of the Eastern community, as Ulbricht said, is an important condition for the quickest possible development of the national economies, and this in turn is necessary if the East is to maintain itself against the West 'in the main field of conflict'.[35]

[34] At the 7th Party Congress (footnote [8]).
[35] Especially informative here are Ulbricht's speeches during the 11th Central Committee meeting (*Neues Deutschland*, 1 August 1969), and at the Moscow world conference, where he spoke in favour of 'the collective wisdom of the whole movement', 'collective working out of common standpoints',

Inside the Warsaw Pact the East German leaders are the most resolute fighters against 'revisionism', 'nationalism' and closer collaboration with the West, in so far as this threatens to bring about economic dependence. Anyone in Eastern Europe who wants reforms or co-operation with Western Europe—and that means every member of the Eastern alliance—has to watch out not only for Moscow but also for East Berlin. The GDR regards as vitally important the greatest caution in reforms and would like, as a Pole once put it, to decide the policy of the whole Warsaw Pact towards West Germany. East Berlin has built up a great deal of activity to achieve this, i.e. to keep the Federal Republic out of Eastern Europe as far as possible. This begins with efforts to secure understanding for East Germany's special position, goes on to economic proposals, and ends up with political pressure. The point at which East German influence becomes interference is sometimes as difficult to define as the boundary between security policy and power politics. Tendencies towards an East German nationalism within Eastern Europe cannot be overlooked.

Methods

(a) Military Policy

In proportion to population the GDR makes available the smallest contingent to the Warsaw Pact.[36] The same is true in absolute terms, apart from the Hungarian army, whose continuing weakness dates from 1956. Even Bulgaria, with just the same population as the GDR, maintains more combat formations than East Germany. This picture alters considerably if one takes into account frontier troops and units for preserving internal security (excluding factory combat groups). Even then the GDR comes only fourth in absolute figures, but relative to its smaller population of military age it comes first.

East Berlin's efforts, then, are at least as great as those of the other Warsaw Pact states, but they are differently distributed. The combat troops, 129,000 strong (including naval and air force personnel), stand alongside 52,500 frontier troops (with full military training) and the 21,000 men of the SED Guard regiment and the police units in barracks. The 'paramilitary' formations (73,500) are therefore more than half as strong as the regular forces (129,000), an imbalance not found anywhere else in the whole Warsaw Pact. In Hungary 'paramilitary' units amount to just over a third of the regular forces, in Rumania to about a quarter and in all the other countries to very much

---

'regular international consultations', 'systematic joint theoretical work', 'agreement in principle on the basic questions and tasks of the anti-imperialist struggle', and 'common actions' in it.

[36] The information in this section rests essentially on *The Military Balance 1969–70*, London: The Institute for Strategic Studies, 1970.

less. This reflects the fact that the numbers in factory combat groups are highest in the GDR, both relatively and absolutely.

The size of the GDR's frontier police is due to the tasks they have to perform. By comparison with the other states of the bloc they have to guard the longest frontier with the 'hostile' West (the Federal Republic and West Berlin) and also to check on surface traffic between West Germany and West Berlin. It is known that these guarding and checking activities are directed less against intrusions from outside than break-outs from within. The structure of East Germany's armed forces illustrates the dilemma of GDR defence. Its politically and geographically exposed position produces such a great internal security requirement that East Berlin can provide only inadequately, and even perhaps not at all, for its *external* security.

This weakness of the GDR's armed forces is not vitally important so long as there are twenty Soviet divisions in the country. But even apart from the possibility of these being reduced or actually withdrawn, it is important for East Berlin to make as great a contribution as possible to its own defence. There are also several other points involved here. An army of its own is *the* status symbol of a sovereign state. A viable, reliably Socialist army creates equality with the other allies. Above all the GDR knows something the South Vietnamese have had to learn— people are only thought worth defending if they make every effort to defend themselves.

These considerations explain why the GDR supports 'complete military integration, total incorporation of national forces and resources into the unitary defence system' of the Warsaw Pact.[37] They explain the efforts to make the national army ideologically impregnable. 'Nearly all officers, half of the NCO's and almost one in nine soldiers are members or candidate members of the SED.' [38] They explain the pride with which Defence Minister Heinz Hoffmann declared in April 1965 that the GDR army formed part of the 'first strategic echelon' of the Pact's forces.[39] They explain the Minister's report to the Seventh Party Congress.[40] Since 1963 national defence had attained 'a new qualitative level' and the army had 'become ever more worthy of the tasks of the Revolution in the military sphere', and was 'today a modern, powerful Socialist army'.

All this however costs a great deal of money and labour. The GDR

---

[37] *Horizont*, April 1969. Compare with the polemic against 'tendencies which overemphasize national peculiarities that no doubt do exist in Socialist military doctrine—which must be regarded, and rejected, as a form of modern revisionism' (*Neues Deutschland*, 23 November 1968).

[38] *Neues Deutschland*, 19 July 1969.

[39] *Neues Deutschland*, 22 April 1965. Cf. Boris Meissner, Jens Hacker, Alexander Uschakow, *Das Paktsystem der Sowjetunion in Osteuropa*, annexe to *Das Parlament*, 12 January 1966.

[40] See footnote [12].

has the shortest period of military service in the Pact, apart from Rumania. This is connected with the numerical weakness of the military age groups and the needs of the economy. On the question of equipment Defence Minister Hoffmann told the Seventh Party Congress that dealing with 'material and technical requirements' in the light of 'new conditions and goals' brought with it a series of problems. It was a matter of securing 'an optimum relationship between the required defence strengths and the highest possible national income'. The modernization of weaponry on which Hoffmann had reported earlier is a burden on East Germany's economy and national budget. Defence expenditures, calculated *per capita* and in relation to national incomes, amount to the following: all the other European allies of the Soviet Union with the exception of Hungary, kept their expenditures on armament steady from 1965 to 1969, or reduced them. In the GDR however there was a massive increase from 3·0 to 5·9 per cent of national income. In 1969 the GDR and Czechoslovakia had the highest military expenditure.

Though East Berlin has a great stake in an effective national defence, the burdens are so great that this must create some interest in lightening them.

(b) Economic Policy

In order to be sure of the Soviet Union and the other allies the GDR has to be efficient economically and technically. Ulbricht has described the connection very clearly:

> An economically powerful, healthy and dynamic GDR . . . mastering the development of the social system of Socialism and the problems of the scientific and technological revolution, in close co-operation and division of labour with the Soviet Union, and making skilful use of the spiritual and material potential of both states and peoples, will become an insuperable bulwark of peace and security in Europe against the West German imperialists.[41]

At the Seventh Party Congress Ulbricht declared that 'external economic relations are one of the basic pillars of our foreign policy'. They had, he said, the greatest importance for the GDR's international position and standing in the world. These principles apply to trade within COMECON, which continues—no doubt for political reasons—to make up 75 per cent of the GDR's total foreign trade, more than for any other COMECON country (except Bulgaria).[42] As is well known, trade as a political instrument plays a decisive part in all

[41] *Neues Deutschland*, 1 August 1969.
[42] Hans Dieter Schulz in *Braucht der Osten die DDR?*, Opladen 1968, pp. 44 ff.

the GDR's efforts to achieve recognition as a state. East Germany, like West Germany, owes its standing among its allies and in the rest of the world above all to its economic strength. For East Berlin, still unrecognized, any gain in international standing means an increase in security.

Still more important is the internal political importance of the economy. For the Socialist countries there are two ways in which they can develop their own version of Socialism and thus to a certain extent reconcile leadership, party and people. They can liberalize or even democratize, as in Czechoslovakia in 1968. Or they can follow a markedly nationalistic policy, as Rumania has done. The East German regime is impeded from doing either. There only remains the option of improving the material conditions of life so far as possible, in order to create a relative contentment. The SED leadership, especially Ulbricht, recognized this in good time and, unlike Novotny in Prague, drew the necessary conclusion firmly. This has enabled them to achieve a degree of internal consolidation that was hardly to be expected in such unfavourable political conditions.

Economic progress was and is more important to the GDR than to other East European states, for both internal and external reasons. For the SED economic policy is much more a matter of security policy than for other Communist Parties.

(c) Home Policy

Just as the external security of the GDR rests on military power, so its internal security is based on the power of the state. This is not to say that the state security service *creates* order in the country, but it does *guarantee* it. Nor is it true to speak of terror as an SED means of government. But this does not exclude the possibility of the Party leadership returning to this method in a crisis, as after the building of the Berlin wall. Only certain knowledge that they have the country permanently under their control, and can call on the most extreme measures in an emergency, gives the leadership confidence that order will be maintained. On the other hand the very existence of these means, and various memories of their application, deters GDR citizens from overstepping certain limits. This conformism is not extorted but occurs of its own accord, because most people will do nothing that might bring them into conflict with the power of the state.

This state of affairs applies to all the Socialist countries, to a greater or lesser extent. The only exception was Czechoslovakia in the first half of 1968—and that proved the rule. The control Dubček dispensed with was restored by others after 21 August. In the GDR in particular there seem to be exaggerated anxieties. Sometimes the disproportion between an incident, such as a mass gathering of modern music fans, and the reaction—large-scale police action and numerous arrests—seems grotesque. In times of tension, such as after the intervention in Czechoslovakia, security measures betray a degree of anxiety that seems out of proportion to the danger. The statement by the television commentator, Schnitzler, that in the GDR the opposition was to be confronted only in the courts[43] is exaggerated, but expresses a basic attitude that continues to exist.

All this however is only the foundation upon which the East German Communists are consolidating their state. Since around 1962 there has been a recognizable policy in which constructive and restrictive elements complement each other. Ulbricht has brought in most reforms in the field where the dangers were least and the expected advantages greatest, in the economy. But where there are movements of intellectual independence, and wider or deeper contact with the West is developing, he firmly refuses to make changes, and brings the trend under strict control or even reverses it. He intervenes energetically if 'revisionist' tendencies appear. This mixture of isolation and welfare produces the GDR version of Socialism. The welfare is intended to take the place of the mitigation of Communism that in other countries is achieved by nationalism, liberalism, slackness and corruption. The isolation is meant to estrange the East Germans from the West, and limit their mental horizon and scope for material comparison to the East.

The 'positive' complement to this is provided by measures intended to demonstrate both the independence and the individual character of the GDR. Further development of the educational system, participation in decisions on technical and local questions, replacing German by GDR citizenship, creating their own penal law and a Socialist constitution, introducing passport and visa requirements for West Germans—all this and much besides forms a large part of the programme of a Socialist state. But it also serves the purpose—in some ways primary—of demonstrating to their own population and to the West alike the unalterable fact of a Socialist German state.

(d) Policy on Germany

Logically as well as ideologically the security of Socialist East Germany requires a Socialist West Germany. But this ultimate conclusion is scarcely reached even theoretically. Apart from chiliastic hopes that

---

[43] 'To oppose our Socialist policy of peace would mean to commit crimes. Crimes against Socialism, crimes against peace, crimes against the people. And such opposition we do not confront at the ballot box or in Parliament but in the law courts of our Socialist justice.'

K. E. v. Schnitzler on the German television programme *Schwarzer Kanal*, 25 April 1968 at 9.15 p.m.

the whole world, including the Federal Republic, will one day become Socialist, East Berlin's wishes and demands in regard to Bonn extend only to the following: the Western, and unfortunately stronger, part of Germany must finally accept the existence of another, differently organized Germany, and recognize its right to life. When it is said in East Berlin that recognition as a state is not the decisive point, this is not a matter of tactics alone. A recognition aimed at promoting liberalization in the GDR looks to the SED leadership simply like a new form of ideological diversion. What they are working for is recognition as an expression of readiness to accept the other side as different, and to treat it as an equal, not only diplomatically but also socially—in every sense of the word. Here psychological and strategic insecurity react upon each other.

The concrete demands East Berlin puts to Bonn are in the last analysis only means to an end. They are meant to guarantee and make credible a change of attitude towards the GDR. The security of the East German state is not to rest on words. It must rest on facts. From this point of view recognition of the GDR plays an important part. In the SED's view it would help to stabilize East Germany internally and externally, by giving international support to the irrevocable nature of the experiment of a Socialist state on German soil.

'Peace and unity in Germany require the exclusion of German imperialists and militarists from power in West Germany.' [44] Whatever this may mean in the concrete, the idea behind this and similar demands lies in the Marxist conviction that only changes in society, the removal from power of groups with an alleged interest in war, can guarantee a peaceful policy. Paradoxical as it may sound, the reason for attitudes like this is more defensive than offensive. But of course it still has to be borne in mind that beyond a certain point defence easily turns into aggression. However, all internal and official statements from East Berlin testify that people are prepared 'for a long period yet' simply to 'live peacefully side by side' with the Federal Republic.[45] The hopelessness of an 'eastward' reunification is thus recognized. A fundamental factor is the desire for certainty that ruling circles in West Germany are really ready to 'leave the GDR in peace'.[46]

[44] Programme of the SED, Part I, Section IV, *Policy for Peace* (*Friedenspolitik*), January 1963.

[45] Ulbricht at the 7th Party Congress (footnote [8]).

[46] This is not contradicted by the much discussed article in *Neues Deutschland*, 23 November 1968, on the military doctrine of the GDR. It is true that this does say that 'for the West German population a war would take on the character of a war of national liberation'. But the precondition for this 'war of national liberation' is that war has been started by West German 'imperialism'. The military doctrine of the GDR here agrees exactly with that of the Soviet Union, as the author of the article emphasizes and as is shown by verbal similarities. In the Soviet view also a war would end with the destruction of

Differences of opinion detectable at the top in the SED relate above all to three questions:

1. How far is a change of opinion in the Federal Republic thinkable or credible?

2. How great are the dangers of 'softening up' arising from negotiations and agreements with Bonn?

3. Which promises more security against these dangers—continued confrontation with West Germany or an arrangement with it?

Hitherto fear and distrust have mostly outweighed readiness to take risks, and the SED leaders' policy has been aimed at creating or preserving the greatest possible distance from the Federal Republic. Thus contacts with West German organizations were only taken up in so far as they promised a gain in prestige or in possible influence within the Federal Republic, without exposure to any significant counter-effects. As soon as this assessment ceased to apply, as in the 1966 exchange of speakers between the SPD and the SED, the SED leaders drew back. At the end of the 1960s their fear of the influence of West German radio and television was still so great that they obstructed objective, non-propagandist reporting on the GDR because West German stations might gain in credibility in the GDR through an accurate depiction of conditions there. On the other hand SED propaganda against the Federal Republic reaches a point at which it can only be explained as intended systematically to discredit Western Germany. For the GDR the bogey of the war-loving *revanchists*, 'militarists' and 'imperialists' is still a substantial part of the justification for its existence. Caution, distrust, keeping one's distance, can only be proclaimed as vitally important so long as the Federal Republic can be denounced as a danger to the peace.

These principles apply also, and particularly, to periods of negotiation between East Berlin and Bonn. When Willi Stoph invited Willy Brandt to a meeting at the beginning of 1970, Erich Honecker simultaneously invoked the allegedly unchanged danger from the Federal Republic—contrary to the opinion of all the other Warsaw Pact states.[47] It is only possible to talk to the West German govern-

---

'imperialism'. But for the Soviet Union a war is only conceivable through escalation of a local conflict or an attack from the West. So the military doctrine of the GDR proves to be no more aggressive than its Soviet model—more exactly, it is the same compromise between defensive policy and aggressive ideology. In addition the East German military have the same national problem as the West Germans. They have to convince their soldiers of the necessity of firing on their compatriots in a crisis.

[47] *Neues Deutschland*, 22 February 1970. That the other Warsaw Pact states judge the Brandt/Scheel Government more favourably is shown by the joint communique following the December 1969 meeting (*Neues Deutschland*, 6 December 1969) and the communiqué after Foreign Minister Gromyko's visit to Berlin at the end of February 1970 (*Neues Deutschland*, 27 February 1970).

ment, it is thought, if one discourages in advance all the hopes which the population and a section of the Party attach to the conversations. At the end of 1970 the SED leaders even evolved a new concept in their policy towards the Federal Republic. In all their speeches and statements they called for 'lines to be drawn' (*Abgrenzung*). Ulbricht summed up the meaning and purpose of this demand: 'When the opponent's policy is aimed at grappling the GDR to himself, the only policy for us is for lines to be drawn resolutely. That is the precondition for an offensive policy of peaceful coexistence towards the Federal Republic.' [48] This means that in times of *détente* its risks can only be borne if one's own party, and state, and camp, have been made stable and immune to *détente's* disintegrating effects.

IV. IDEAS AND PROSPECTS FOR THE FUTURE

Disarmament and European Security

Statements by the GDR Government on disarmament and security in Europe since the mid-1950s fall into three categories:[49]

1. Support for proposals from their own camp, above all the Soviet Union, Poland and the Warsaw Pact.

2. Proposals for arms limitation, disarmament and neutralization in the two German states.

3. Proposals including or aimed at Western recognition of the GDR as an equal, sovereign state.

Statements in the first category are not original, while those in the second are nearly always not serious, since they relate only to Germany. Reduction of military forces by half, removal of nuclear weapons, or similar proposals, if carried out only in the Federal Republic and GDR, would damage the East–West balance in Europe and with it the preconditions for any disarmament agreement. It must be clear to the East Berlin leaders that such proposals have no prospect of being accepted.

East Berlin's only contribution of its own on the subject of European security lies in the demand that equal rights for East Germans be a condition of any European security arrangement. For the rest the attitude of the East German leadership is determined by three points:

1. Preservation of Soviet protection;

2. Precautions against closer contact with West Germany;

3. Weakening the Federal Republic.

Thus the GDR is keenly interested in an American withdrawal

[48] *Neues Deutschland*, 14 January 1971.

[49] A useful collection of documents up to autumn 1967 is provided by *Sicherheit und friedliche Zusammenarbeit in Europa*, Staatsverlag der DDR, Berlin 1968.

from Europe. The Western argument that NATO restrains West German activity is not believed in. And the idea of some East Europeans that the United States constitutes a valuable counter-weight to excessive Soviet power seems to carry no weight in East Berlin, so far at any rate. To the East German Communists it seems to be the other way round—only the American alliance makes Bonn dangerous. The GDR need not be afraid of the Federal Republic on its own, either militarily or politically, so long as the Soviet Union stands by it. On the other hand Washington might oblige Moscow to accept restraints or compromises, by means of military support or economic assistance for Bonn's Eastern policy. The more it is possible to weaken the American commitment, especially the American link with Bonn, and to isolate the Federal Republic in Western Europe, the more secure the GDR feels.

There is scarcely any discussion in the GDR of the price of an American withdrawal, dissolution of the Warsaw Pact and withdrawal of Soviet troops. People do indeed stand by the line laid down at the conferences in Bucharest, Karlovy Vary and Budapest, but with the greatest possible reserve. Statements by Deputy Foreign Minister Peter Florin are very characteristic in this respect.[50] In 123 pages devoted to the GDR's foreign policy he gives precisely *one* to the dissolution of military alliances. It does not strike him as a demand or a necessity, but as a 'problem'. The objective to be reached is abolition of the 'aggressive' NATO. The readiness of the Warsaw Pact states for simultaneous dissolution of both alliances is only mentioned in order to draw the conclusion that so long as NATO exists, 'especially the Washington-Bonn axis', the Socialist countries 'have no option but to strengthen their defensive alliance'. This is followed by an appropriate quotation from the Bucharest declaration.

Florin also deals with the subject of 'agreed disarmament' in scarcely more than a page, and in the same style of 'yes—but'. Eastern suggestions are cited, culminating in the statement that 'in all these proposals account has to be taken of the real situation in Europe and the danger of war arising from an armed West Germany'. Then follows the section on withdrawal of troops from the GDR quoted on p. 20.[51]

[50] *Op. cit.* (footnote 8), pp. 117–19.
[51] It is worth noting that Florin cites the Karlovy Vary and not the Bucharest disarmament proposals. The Bucharest declaration specifies 'withdrawal of all foreign troops from other countries to within their national frontiers'. The Karlovy Vary conference called for 'the withdrawal of foreign troops from the territory of European states'.

The first formula definitely includes the Russians. The second does not exclude them, but could be interpreted as applying to the withdrawal of troops foreign to Europe, i.e. the Americans. That Florin uses the Karlovy Vary version is of course not due to chance, any more than the way he deals with

Thus the GDR regards the dissolution of the military alliances with the greatest reserve, and would like to avoid a withdrawal of Soviet troops for as long as possible. If these two measures are not regarded as a unity, as is usually assumed, then the picture is changed. A dissolution of the Warsaw Pact, but with Soviet divisions remaining in the GDR (for which a legal basis could be found) would be bound to look attractive to East Berlin. It would probably loosen the cohesion of the former NATO states more than the ties between the northern countries of the Warsaw Pact. In addition, an all-European security system would give East Germany, not indeed full recognition, but equal rights as a European state.

For Soviet troops to leave the GDR is regarded in East Berlin as worth considering only on three conditions, as Florin says or implies:

1. All foreign troops must leave the Federal Republic at the same time.

2. The *Bundeswehr*, like the *Volksarmee*, must simultaneously be disarmed to an agreed extent.

3. Bilateral military alliances with the Soviet Union and other Socialist countries—at least with Poland and Czechoslovakia—must be maintained. The same applies to economic and political connections with these countries.

Towards the end of the 1950s East Berlin may have had reservations about Polish plans for a nuclear-free zone in Central Europe. But now that such a plan can no longer take any account of Bonn's reservations on non-recognition, the GDR can expect more advantages than disadvantages from it. In East Berlin's view Bonn's acquisition, or even sharing, of nuclear weapons, which acceptance of the Polish plan would prevent, is the decisive step that would give the West German *revanchists* the ability and confidence to threaten militarily the GDR and other Socialist countries.[52]

To keep the *Bundeswehr* away from weapons of mass destruction has been and is East Berlin's main objective in the sphere of arms-control agreements. This can be seen in the GDR's proposals at the end of the 1950s, in harmony with Soviet policy, which practically speaking anticipated for Germany the Non-Proliferation Treaty of 1968. It was repeated in endless polemics, including support for the treaty 'so far as it in fact fulfils what is expected, i.e. above all preventing access by the imperialists of West Germany to nuclear

---

the Bucharest declaration. It is well known that the text of this was much more strongly influenced than the Karlovy Vary declaration by forces within the Pact interested in *détente* and settlement. But Florin in his book only quotes from it the passages dealing with demands upon the Federal Republic, and with the defensive efforts of the Eastern Alliance.

[52] This view becomes particularly clear in Ulbricht's speech at the 7th Party Congress.

weapons in any form'.[53] East Berlin's second desire in the disarmament field seems to be for the Federal Republic to be cleared of foreign nuclear weapons. Peter Florin suggests an addition to this effect to the Non-Proliferation Treaty,[54] and several drafts from the 1950s aimed at the same thing.

So long as the two super-powers do not withdraw their troops from Germany, the GDR would probably feel more secure in a nuclear-free zone than at present. Such a zone would have to contain installations for verification that would further restrict Bonn's military freedom of manœuvre. Finally it would bring the same political gain as a security system. The GDR, as part of such a zone, would not be recognized unconditionally in international law, but would still become a full and equal Central European state.

Problems could only arise for East Berlin if there was a question not only of arms limitations but also of a 'zone of peace and co-operation' such as was suggested in Karlovy Vary in 1967 and seems to have been considered again in Warsaw in 1969. The co-operation with the Federal Republic this would involve would again confront the SED leaders with the whole series of ideological and political dangers which they have only with difficulty avoided since 1967. They would have to take into account possible West German influences, not only on the GDR but also on Poland and Czechoslovakia—a really serious prospect for part at least of the East German leadership, even though internal recognition of the GDR formed a precondition of such a co-operative zone.

Little can be learnt from the GDR about the form of a 'system of collective security'. What has been written about it follows the pattern of Soviet proposals of the 1950s, in which each country is to guarantee each against all. The main problem in this pattern—how far the old blocs would survive or, in a crisis, re-form within the common framework—does not seem to be discussed. Finally it is an important interest of the GDR that the Eastern bloc be preserved as completely as possible.[55]

The GDR is Europe's least 'European' state. Until a few years ago

---

[53] Florin, op. cit. (footnote 8), p. 121.   [54] Op. cit. (footnote 8), p. 120.

[55] Only two things seem to be worth noting in East Berlin statements about a security system. First, the emphasis on the 'sovereign equality' that the system must guarantee. And secondly some uncertainty so far as the preservation of the internal order is concerned. On the one hand such a system should 'leave it to the peoples of each European state to determine their own political and social order—free from aggression and intervention'. On the other hand, however, it should only guarantee 'external' security and not make it possible 'to shelter the social structure of a particular state from the action of internal forces'. (Dokumentation [note 49], pp. 327; 22/3). What is wanted is to bind others but not oneself. So far as the GDR is concerned, with its main problem of relations with the Federal Republic, there can be little doubt that the defensive aspect is more important than the offensive.

the word 'European' hardly existed in the SED's vocabulary. Any reference to 'European' prospects for the Germans ran into incomprehension or distrust in East Berlin. No Polish, Czech, Hungarian or Rumanian politician would have made a *faux pas* such as Ulbricht perpetrated in the summer of 1968, when he said of Bonn's Eastern policy; 'With the help of "liberalization" in the peoples' democracies . . . conditions are to be created for the hegemony of West German imperialism not only over Europe, but up to the Bug.'[56] This is the old Bonn usage of 'Europe' to mean Western Europe! That Ulbricht slipped into it shows that the East German Communists have no idea of their own of a future Europe. All they know is the European (i.e. *West* European) policy of Bonn, which seems to them dangerous, and the Socialist camp. While Poland, Hungary and Rumania, and in 1968 Czechoslovakia also, developed and in part realized concepts in which national interests fitted in with the requirements of all-European security, East Berlin never got beyond dressing up the wishes of the GDR in European guise.

The SED remains hung up on its own problems, above all West Germany. In 1970 it is still at the stage in which the Federal Republic was up to the middle of the 1960s. It would like to make its objectives into preconditions for any European conference or settlement, and accepts only with difficulty the idea that *détente* in Europe is also a precondition, and a way, for the GDR to be accepted as an equal state throughout the continent.

Normalization of the GDR

Up to the beginning of the 1960s most Western observers regarded the problem of the GDR as insoluble. But since then developments have appeared which, in defiance of all the theories, are partly creating and partly promise to create a state that will be viable without a great deal of external support. As always it is a question of one's point of view. If East Germany is compared with the other Warsaw Pact states, what stands out is what is not normal in this artificially created structure. But if one compares the GDR of 1970 with that of 1960 or 1955, it becomes apparent how much has already been normalized. It is possible to detect a consolidation which advances only slowly, is disrupted in many ways and by no means quite safe from disaster, but seems likely to make steady progress. In October 1969 the GDR reached its twentieth anniversary. That is six years more than the Weimar Republic and eight years longer than Hitler's Third Reich.

A new generation is growing up.[57] A poll of East German school-

[56] *Neues Deutschland*, 21 June 1968.
[57] I owe the details that follow to Herr Ruprecht Eser, whose as yet unpublished book on youth research in the GDR I have been able to see in manuscript.

children aged 14 to 16 found that less than five per cent of the boys and only two and a half per cent of the girls regarded the reunification of Germany as important. However, for only four per cent of the boys and three per cent of the girls was the GDR's future in the forefront of their expectations either. Professional success, leisure, art, love, family, marriage and travel ranked far above the 'causes' that, according to the ideas and wishes of the ruling generation in East and West Germany alike, ought to move young people. With regard to the Federal Republic the SED seems to have succeeded in implanting certain prejudices. For secondary schoolboys (but not the technical school pupils who are less indoctrinated), Soviet citizens are the 'most peace-loving' while suitable descriptions of the West Germans, apart from 'modern', are felt to be 'aggressive', 'arrogant', 'egoistic', 'imperious'. It is true that in the oath of dedication for youth each has to undertake to 'guard the peace and defend Socialism against every imperialist attack'. But of the schoolchildren questioned (in the first poll), only six per cent considered the peace to be in danger. 'War is not regarded by our boys and girls as an immediately threatening danger, destroying all personal wishes and efforts.' More frequently there are complaints that the dangerous nature of the enemy is under-estimated.[58] As the director of the Leipzig *Zentralinstitut für Jugend-forschung* writes, 'Tolerance in the wrong sphere'—i.e. towards the West—is 'not sufficiently combatted', while the weaknesses of one's own side are viewed 'harshly and without restraint'.

The coming of a new generation will perhaps play a still larger part in the GDR than in other Warsaw Pact countries. The fifty- and sixty-year-olds who have fought or endured the strenuous battle for the existence and rights of their state will probably never completely lose their excessive caution, a constant feeling of mistrust in all directions, and a residual insecurity. The younger age groups, whose picture of the world has been formed wholly or mainly in and by the GDR, show more self-confidence, in so far as they take for granted what older people regard as hard-won gains. Nevertheless even for the East German Communists the time of life-and-death anxiety is over. For the GDR today, subjectively and objectively, it is no longer a question of to be or not to be, but of winning or losing positions that offer a gain or loss in security. Formerly East Berlin's strength consisted in its weakness, which everyone had to take into account. Now East Germany disposes of some natural strength of its own and has prospects of acquiring more. The GDR has come of age, as Ulbricht said in the late summer of 1969.[59] Part of its difficulties are bound up with this change from being an object to becoming a subject of policy, as is also the contradictory picture it still presents.

[58] For example *Neues Deutschland*, 30 August 1969.
[59] *Neues Deutschland*, 1 August 1969.

Even after international recognition, considerations of security will still be an essential determining factor in the policy of the East Berlin Government, and its concept of security will change only gradually, and not in fundamentals. Support from the Soviet Union will continue to be the basis of all GDR policies. But there may be a growing inclination to complement guarantees from the East by a settlement with the West. The speed and extent of such changes depend on how quickly and how far the internal consolidation of the GDR continues. The main danger for the East German state, and still more for the dominance of the largely conservative top party leadership, is ideological. The main salvation from it is promised by economic growth. The higher the standard of living—so East Berlin calculates—the less need to fear the Western example, the greater the chances of showing Eastern 'revisionists' a GDR model of welfare Socialism, the more the possibility, too, of further stabilization by cautious liberalization.

The security of the GDR, then, increases to the extent that the East German state establishes itself. Only when the leadership and party élite lose their feeling of insecurity at home, which is partly justified and partly not, can they develop a feeling of security abroad. Subjective and objective facts here coincide. Even conservative West German politicians are ready today to accept that there are two states in Germany, so long as they can believe that East Germans are content with their own state and regime.

POLAND

A United Socialist Germany? We don't want to
commit suicide.   (A Pole, 1969)

I. LESSONS AND CONSEQUENCES OF THE WAR

The German 'Drang nach Osten'

Poland lies on the 'everlasting strategic route of the imperialistic
Germanic drive to the East'. But it also lies 'on the way from Moscow
to Berlin', and from every point of view it lies 'in the area of direct
contact between two political systems, the nerve point of the whole
international situation'.[1] Many passages of this kind could be cited,
and the word 'geopolitics' plays a greater part in discussions of
security in Warsaw than elsewhere. The Poles live, without natural
frontiers, between the Russians and the Germans. The result has been
that their frontiers to East and West have mostly remained unclear,
insecure and disputed. Above all, though Poland was occasionally
able to expand at the expense of its neighbours, during the last two
centuries its fate has depended largely on the relationship between
Russians and Germans. When they fought, this happened in Poland;
when they agreed, it was at Poland's expense. After its four historic
partitions, the country suffered between 1939 and 1945 every conceivable misfortune, one after the other: It was conquered and divided
by both Russians and Germans and completely occupied by the
Germans. Then it became a battlefield between the Russians and the
Germans and was finally completely occupied by the Russians.

Despite considerable transformations in the political scenery, the
situation has changed only a little since the war. Poland has indeed
been drawn into the East-West division of the world, but its two
principal opponents each play a role, perhaps even the decisive role, in
their own camp. And so today too Poland's fate is determined essentially
if less than before, by the relationship of its two great neighbours to
each other and to Warsaw.[2] Although the GDR forms the frontier area
of the Warsaw Pact, the Poles are in no doubt that any future conflict

---

[1] Prime Minister Cyrankiewicz (as quoted in *Neue Zürcher Zeitung*, 19 July
1969); *Zycie Warszawy*, mid-January 1969, reprinted in *Polish Perspectives*,
May 1969, p. 3; Chairman of the State Council Spychalski, 9 April 1969 at a
meeting of the All-Polish Committee of the National Unity Front.

[2] *Zycie Warszawy, op. cit.*

between Russians and Germans, between the Warsaw Pact and NATO, would hit their country hard. This applies not only to the eventuality of war, but also to periods of great political tension.

The first conclusion that follows for all Poles from the history of the past few decades is an elementary one. Every nation that experienced the last war is afraid of the very idea of another. But in so far as this fear exists to a special degree, it is to be found in Poland. The country which had to go through more than any other between 1939 and 1945 is today dominated more than any other by the idea of security.

Warsaw also draws from the more recent past three political lessons in the narrow sense:[3]

1. The German occupation up to 1944 was the worst Poland had suffered in all its history. But to a people conscious of a thousand-year-old German 'drive to the East', this oppression seems extraordinary only in its extent. In the Polish view Hitler stands in a Prussian-German tradition that flows consistently from the partitions of the eighteenth and nineteenth centuries through Bismarck's efforts at Germanization to the struggle for the revision of the Versailles Treaty. The 'dogma of this policy' was the 'destruction of the Polish state'. Hitler only did what 'nationalist and militarist Germany' had always done or tried to do. It is true, people do distinguish in Poland between Hitlerites and Germans, but the Hitlerites were of course German, and besides, there were a great many of them. While the Germans themselves are today inclined for the most part to try to put the blame on Hitler personally, on the regime and on very small groups in the leadership, in Poland the opposite tendency prevails, pointedly expressed as follows: 'In our experience there were a handful of German anti-fascists and liberals against a mass of murderers.'[4]

This view of history leads irresistibly to conclusions about the present. An historical current that is so ancient, widespread and powerful cannot quickly and completely disappear. Extreme vigilance and the greatest security precautions against the Germans are therefore necessary.

2. Poland's distrust has been strengthened by its experiences with France and Britain during the 1920s and 1930s. In Warsaw today people are often not content merely to assert that the Western powers were unable to save Poland, despite their guarantee and declaration of war in 1939. It is suspected that they did not wish to do so, or did not wish it with sufficient resolution. The sequence of reproaches begins with the Treaty of Locarno which confirmed only the Western

[3] The following owes a good deal to the paper presented in September 1969 by Ryszard Wojna, deputy editor of *Zycie Warszawy*, at an international conference for journalists at Jablonna, near Warsaw. The manuscript has only been mimeographed.

[4] The writer Tadeusz Holnj, 2 September 1969. (*PAP Daily News*, No. 245.)

boundaries of Germany and left the Eastern open—'Food for revenge-seekers, for militarists and finally for Hitler's military, genocidal plans,' as Prime Minister Cyrankiewicz has said.[5]

The reasons for the French and British policy which created or allowed free passage to Hitler are identified in Warsaw as follows:

(a) a willingness for peace at any price, especially when others have to pay for it;

(b) an underestimation of the dangers that arose from Germany;

(c) a susceptibility to German propaganda, according to which an injustice was done to Germany at Versailles;

(d) hostility to the Soviet Union extending to the hope of diverting German activity to the East.[6]

To many Poles the last three at least of these four points seem to be valid today (so much so that the present might even to some small extent have influenced their view of the past). Thus Prime Minister Cyrankiewicz saw 'short-sightedness or even cynicism' among 'those politicians in the West who have been pumping thousands of millions of dollars . . . into West Germany . . . and misleading the public by nourishing the fantasy that the Federal Republic would give up its expansionist intentions if it became a prosperous country'. In another passage the Polish Head of Government said that 'aggressive German imperialism' had been 'resurrected after the war by the Western powers in a new attack of their anti-Communist obsession'.[7]

3. Some of the West's mistakes are also to be seen, from the present Warsaw viewpoint, in their own pre-war government—hostility to the Soviet Union, an underestimation of the German danger, and the 'dishonourable stain' of participation in the liquidation of Czechoslovakia in 1939. The cause of Poland's misfortune was the 'theory of the two enemies', the attempt to steer between the Soviet Union and Germany with the result that both united against Poland.

Allowing for a certain one-sidedness in this picture, it can be said that these three areas of experience are almost universal in Poland today. Visitors, and still more permanent observers, can confirm that mistrust of the Germans lies very deep, right down to the generation

[5] In a speech of 23 May 1969.

[6] The main reasons advanced to support this view are: France's passivity when Hitler occupied the demilitarized Rhineland in 1936; the delivery of Czechoslovakia to Germany instead of resisting, together with the Soviet Union, Hitler's demands; losing the 'irrevocable opportunity of attacking the Nazi aggressor' at a time when 'the bulk of his forces were involved in the war against Poland, and Germany's Western frontiers were almost unprotected' (Wojna, *op. cit.*). A more differentiated presentation, particularly of French and British policy, is given by Jerzy Krasuski in *Polish Perspectives*, December 1968, p. 58.

[7] In an interview given to *Neue Zeit* (Moscow) on the occasion of the New Year, 1969.

that experienced the war and the occupation only as children. Similarly everyone knows that in an emergency no help is to be expected from the West. Poland does not lie in the Western powers' sphere of interest, either economically or politically, and each country follows its own *raison d'état*, not that of other countries, as *Zycie Warszawy* wrote in January 1969.[8] Finally it seems obvious that a country in Poland's geopolitical position cannot afford a policy of 'balance'.

The conclusion from all this is inescapable. So as not to become once more the victim of joint German-Soviet action, Poland must tie its future firmly to one of its two neighbours—and in the nature of things this can only be the Soviet Union. When a choice first became necessary, in 1945, no real decision was possible, since Germany no longer existed and Poland had come into the Soviet power zone. This meant that any later decision was also to a large extent excluded in advance. However the choice of their Eastern neighbour also corresponded to the feeling in the country since—despite the Katyn massacre and the similar fate of the Polish Communist Party leadership—their experience of the Germans was worse than of the Russians. As the unofficial but current formula puts it—'The Russians only want to rule over us; the Germans wanted to wipe us out as a nation.'

Something like one in every six Polish citizens, more than six million in all, did not survive the war period. But only a small part (about ten per cent) were victims of military action. The majority, especially members of the intelligentsia, died in accordance with a plan of extermination, or as a result of barbaric conditions that were to some extent part of this plan. The 'destruction of Poland', not only as a state but as a nation, the 'abolition of its vital force', the condemnation of its population to be 'slaves of the greater German Reich' in a 'gigantic labour camp'—these declared aims of Hitler and his followers,[9] and their partial realization, are bound to be, for Poles, a memory that overrides everything else and conditions their thinking as it does their politics. Whatever Stalin did to them before and after 1945—in comparison with what Hitler did and planned the Soviet divisions in 1944 brought them liberation.

The Oder–Neisse Line

The second historical datum that conditions Poland's thinking on security derives from the territorial changes and re-groupings of population during 1945–6. Apart from Germany no country in Europe has suffered transformations on this scale. Millions of Poles were transplanted from the former Polish Eastern provinces to the West, mostly

[8] See footnote [1].
[9] Martin Broszat: *Nationalsozialistische Polenpolitik 1939–1954*, Stuttgart 1961, p. 9.

into the former German Eastern provinces, and the Germans living there were driven out to the West. In Warsaw today these proceedings are regarded, in retrospect at least, as a consistent, if indeed radical, application of ethnic principles. To East and West alike they eliminated the causes of conflict created by frontier areas of mixed population and by national minorities. They made it possible 'to establish Polish–Soviet relations on a new, firm basis, consisting not only of the same ideology, but also of common national interests'.[10]

One-third of the present area of the Polish state was formerly German. The Poles justify this acquisition both by their sufferings and by their achievements: 'The Polish nation has paid for them [the newly-acquired territories] a high price in blood, suffering and loss during the second world war.' [11] The second reason is historical—it is said to be a question of regaining original Polish soil, an act of decolonization. Both arguments may be challenged, but to the Poles they appear to be of vital importance. The question whether or how far Poland has an economic need for the 'Northern and Western districts' is hardly more than an academic exercise for economists venturing into politics or, more generally, politicians playing at economics.[12] By contrast, the question of the state's territorial integrity is closely, and probably inseparably, linked with the integration of Poland as a state and nation. A nation that for two hundred years has been partitioned, conquered, suppressed, treated as inferior and regarded as incapable of forming a state, and finally threatened with permanent slavery and extermination needs certainties upon which to support itself internally and externally. History provides the spiritual rallying point for all Poles, Communists and non-Communists alike. No country in Europe has gone so far in rebuilding ruined cities exactly as they were before as Poland, which suffered the greatest material damage. The second unifying common factor lies in the struggles and experiences of the last war.

Poland's territory supplies the practical basis for its future. However, the immutability of the Western frontier is not a territorial claim but a vital need. Mid-twentieth century Poland is the Poland established between the Oder–Neisse and the Bug. It has taken possession of this territory, developed it and rebuilt its cities. Anyone or anything threatening this state of affairs which, though favourable, was achieved by heavy suffering, seems to threaten the existence of Poland itself.

[10] Andrzej Jezierski, *Polish Perspectives*, January 1969.

[11] Gomulka, 21 July 1969, on the occasion of the twenty-fifth anniversary of the Polish People's Republic.

[12] The Polish position is: 'Without the border on the Oder and the Lausitz Neisse Poland would not be viable as a state. The Western districts amount to a third of our country's territory, are inhabited by a fourth of our population and produce more than a third of the state's total production' (*Slowo Powszechne*, 15 May 1969)

Thus the frontier question is *the* national question for the whole country.

II. DANGERS

Danger of War

'The most important question of our age is still the problem of war and peace.' So Gomulka told the Moscow Conference of Communist Parties in June 1969. Similar quotations can be taken from almost all the statesmen of Eastern Europe, but in Poland this assertion seems to be not only more frequent but more emphatic. It is true that no responsible politician in Warsaw reckons on a deliberate world war. But people do not exclude a nuclear catastrophe through accident, negligence, escalation, or the extension of a local war on another continent. Europe seems here to be especially threatened, because of the military concentration of the two blocs. Gomulka has said that the danger of a local conflict becoming an 'atomic war with unforeseeable consequences' is here 'a hundred times greater' than elsewhere.[13]

In the autumn of 1969 the Director of the Warsaw Institute for International Affairs, Ryszard Frelek, pointed to two 'main causes of danger'—'the division of our continent into two powerful military groupings' and the 're-militarization of the Federal Republic of Germany'.[14] On the first point Frelek brings forward well-known arguments which are also current in Poland: 'Lasting peace cannot rest upon armaments which involve permanent rivalry in "nuclear readiness".' 'Peace cannot be built upon a "balance of terror", if only because such a "balance" can be upset one day, or because someone might come to believe it had changed in his favour. Under conditions of "armed peace" any serious provocation may call forth an explosion.' Certainly, as Frelek explicitly says, both military alliances have so far behaved in a peaceful manner, and in the summer of 1969 Gomulka drew attention to a unique event in the modern history of Europe—a quarter-century without war. He added, however, that this did not mean 'that peace has finally been secured in our continent'.[15] The view of the political élite in Warsaw can be defined as follows: There is no immediate danger of war, but there is still no guarantee of lasting peace.

[13] At the Karlovy Vary Conference of the European Communist Parties in April 1967.

[14] At the conference of journalists in Jablonna (footnote 3). The manuscript is only available in mimeographed form.

[15] At the ceremonial meeting of the *Sejm* on the occasion of the twenty-fifth anniversary of the Polish Peoples' Republic, 21 July 1969.

Dangers in the West

The second 'main cause of danger' is reflected in Poland's treaties of mutual assistance with other Socialist states. The only opponent specified is 'West German militarism and revanchism'.[16] In the treaties with the Soviet Union, Czechoslovakia and the GDR, that is to say the politically most important agreements, the parties undertake 'to render impossible an aggression by the forces of West German militarism and *revanchism*, or of any other state or group of states which enters into an alliance with these forces'.[17] The obligation of military assistance applies only to an 'armed attack' by a state or group of states falling within this definition. This limitation is to be found only in the three *Polish* treaties. The Warsaw Pact, like all agreements for mutual assistance, provides for military assistance among its members against an attack by *any* state and *any* group of states.

The limitation in scope of the Polish treaties becomes still clearer if one considers that they do not speak of the Federal Republic and its allies but of the 'forces of West German militarism and *revanchism*', and of states that ally themselves with these 'forces'. Here it is not the existing Western alliance that appears as the possible aggressor but a future, perhaps merely *de facto* alliance that warmongering groups in Bonn might form with other Western governments (the treaties with Moscow and Prague even use the *subjunctive* here). Thus it is presupposed, first, that 'militarists and revanchists' have complete power in Bonn—whether this is already the case the treaty texts leave open—and secondly, that they find some support for their militarist, expansionist plans in other NATO capitals.

The picture of the enemy given in the Polish military treaties corresponds to the historical experiences already described and to the statements of politicians and the press. 'NATO is judged by every Pole according to its policy towards Germany,' Foreign Minister Rapacki told the United Nations as early as 2 October 1957. For Poland the Germans are the danger. Other West Europeans become dangerous only as their accomplices, if through naïveté, short-sightedness or anti-Communist prejudice they support the Germans instead of keeping them on a leash, as would serve their own best interests. Indeed, in the Polish view the British, French and others have come to be aware of these interests and will become even more so, the more the Federal Republic gains in influence. Thus the West Europeans are gradually coming to look to the Poles more like potential allies than potential opponents. A good indication of this has been, among others,

---

[16] The only exception is the treaty with distant Bulgaria which is directed against the 'forces' of 'imperialism' and 'revanchism'.
[17] This is the formula used in the treaty between Poland and the GDR.

the number of commentaries that attributed the Federal Government's open attitude towards Eastern Europe to Bonn's fear of becoming isolated in Western Europe through its rigid Eastern policy.[18] Besides, not only is it known in Warsaw that the West Europeans regard the Oder–Neisse border as final, but there are occasional speculations that Bonn's allies might press Bonn to recognize this frontier, and might even succeed in bringing this about.

The above also applies, with some reservation, to the United States. The reservation refers above all to the strongly ideologically conditioned section of the leadership which sees the Americans primarily as the 'principal power of imperialism' and still hears echoes of the call for 'liberation' in the 1950s. At that time the United States, as Gomulka puts it, was following 'a policy of liquidating Socialism or at least of forcing Socialism back within the frontiers of the USSR'.[19] But this is ancient history now. At the Fourth Party Congress in June 1964, for example, the Polish Communist leader distinguished between 'militarist circles' and 'far-sighted' people in Washington. The first group had not yet given up the idea of a 'hot' war against the Socialist camp, while the others saw clearly the dangerous consequences of atomic weapons in the hands of the West German army. Even in 1969 there was still talk of the 'aggressive circles' and 'aggressive policy' of the United States,[20] but no responsible person in Warsaw entertains any doubt of the deterrent effect of the nuclear balance.[21] One does not even hear much about the 'Washington–Bonn axis' in Poland. On the other hand, there is some doubt whether the Americans are really willing or able to 'tame' the West Germans.

Among the population opinion seems to have developed in the opposite direction. The large number of Americans of Polish origin has made the dollar almost a second legal currency in Poland. But the high esteem for America, bordering on idealization, which used to express itself in enthusiastic receptions for American politicians has grown less with the Vietnam war. Unprejudiced thinkers among the political élite see the United States for what it is, a world power with all the dangers and possibilities that this implies. For years Washington's war in Vietnam has been an obstacle to East–West agreement in Europe. On the other hand, it would be greatly to the advantage of Poland in particular if Washington were to try for agreement with Eastern Europe. All groups, however, make one crucial distinction— the Germans have made claims on Poland, while to the Americans

[18] See, for instance, *Zycie Warszawy*, 4 June 1969.

[19] At the Karlovy Vary Conference of European Communist Parties in April 1967.

[20] See, for instance, the election programme of the National Unity Front (Radio Warsaw I, 9 April 1969).

[21] For example, Gomulka at the Karlovy Vary Conference of Communist Parties in April 1967, or in his speech of 17 May 1969.

Poland is a matter of indifference. There can only be a conflict with them if East and West as a whole come into conflict.

Relations with West Germany

The main source of danger continues to be the Germans, first and foremost the West Germans. Officially, all mistrust is directed against them. In 1949 the GDR had no choice but to give formal recognition to the fact that about a quarter of the former area of the German Reich was now part of Poland. The Federal Republic refused recognition and this, combined with its claim to speak for the whole of Germany, called in question a third of Poland's national territory. On the Polish side there was a corresponding insecurity which even now, at the end of the 1960s, does not seem to have altogether disappeared. The continued use of the term 'Northern and Western districts' to describe the new territories, as if they were a *special* part of the country may be a symptom of this. So too is the emphasis with which the immutability of the Oder–Neisse frontier is repeatedly stressed. In actual fact these former German provinces are now not only almost completely settled with Poles but have merged with the rest of Poland.

In retrospect the exchanges concerning the Oder–Neisse frontier leave the impression that both sides embarked on a senseless escalation. The West Germans, by denying recognition, provoked Polish demands for it, and these in turn stiffened the West Germans in their refusal. What originally arose out of a real Polish fear and, for a time, a firm belief on the part of many Germans, gradually turned into a question of prestige for both. By the time they realized that this frontier was immutable and fears and hopes alike had lost all basis, both Poles and West Germans had become prisoners of their own domestic politics.

The continuing political effect of this pointless dispute has been above all that the post-war period has confirmed or seemed to confirm judgments and prejudices formed during the war. For the Poles (the only people who count in this connection) there is too much in West Germany that feeds their historically-based distrust. On the frontier question many officials of 'expellee' organizations express themselves quite plainly, while many politicians are ambiguous. The second fact is and always has been worse than the first. It is understandable that there should be incorrigibles. But that people in responsible positions should agree with them and finance them out of public funds aroused suspicion in Warsaw that the West German government is secretly supporting what it cannot itself put forward publicly. It is the same with the NPD. What the Poles consider so significant is not the existence of this Party, nor its limited electoral success, but the attitude of democratic politicians—of Federal Chancellor Kiesinger who wanted to free the right-wing radicals from the odium of right-wing radicalism, and of some Social Democrats who tried to justify their own caution on the frontier question by pointing to the NPD. The Polish answer was to point to the alternatives: either the swing to the right, contrary to West German reassurances, was today strong enough to be a decisive obstacle to Bonn's policy and tomorrow would probably control it, or the speeches about the NPD were only excuses to conceal their own intentions.

But these are only some examples. The suspicion that the Germans do not really mean it when they talk about 'reconciliation' rests especially on the fact that Warsaw's proposals for Europe, above all for regional arms limitation, have evoked no response from Bonn.[22] This disappointment at the failure of years of repeated effort is deep-seated. What German critics have attributed to Bonn's ideological fear of Communism and inability to understand events east of the Elbe looks to the Poles like ill will. In 1969 people in Warsaw were still asking: 'What are you waiting for, if you will not recognize the Oder–Neisse frontier and give no reply to our proposals for disarmament or for a conference, or reply only hesitantly and evasively, trying to shrug them off? If our plans are no good or need to be supplemented, why do you not supplement them or draw up something better?'

Such statements express more than a distrust of hidden political reservations. The Poles' relations with the West Germans are complicated by their contradictory feelings towards the West as a whole, which at once attracts and alarms them. They know that despite all the progress they have made in their own development, they are still lagging a long way behind Western Europe, and this shows, in relation to the Federal Republic, in a mixture of resentment, admiration and anxiety. Resentment because the nation that held back Poland's development for decades is becoming richer and stronger all the time, as if it had won the war; admiration because the Germans recovered so quickly despite their annihilating defeat in 1945; and anxiety because they know from experience that German industry can cause as much harm as good.

It is true that Warsaw has noted since as long ago as the end of the 1950s—though with some interruptions—that there are voices in the Federal Republic seeking reconciliation with Poland by recognition of the results of World War II. In 1969 a new evaluation of West German conditions was detectable. The Warsaw periodical *Kultura* spoke of a 'qualitatively new situation' based on a 'development . . . among certain circles in West Germany . . . where Poland is recognized and respected'.[23] The 'realistic' forces are favourably mentioned

[22] For greater detail see Hansjakob Stehle: *Nachbar Polen*, new enlarged edition, Frankfurt am Main. 1968, p. 295.

[23] No. 22/1969.

everywhere and even the harshness in the speeches of the leaders of the 'expellees' is no longer attributed to their strength but, correctly, to their increasing weakness.[24] On the whole what Polish experts on West Germany see is a polarization of opinion into growing realism and growing nationalism, cause both for increased hopes and increased fears in Warsaw.

For the Poles the signing of the Warsaw treaty by Federal Chancellor Brandt was a victory for 'realistic forces'. By this treaty the Federal Republic of Germany confirmed that Poland's Western frontier was final. The formal reservations still contained in the treaty seemed tolerable to Warsaw because they were only formal, a necessary result of the legal position of the Federal Republic, and not political. The decisive factor here was the personal trust won by Brandt in Poland. The Poles believed in his desire for agreement. After his visit to Warsaw he was said to be the first Western politician since de Gaulle who understood completely Poland's position.

The treaty's importance for Poland can hardly be exaggerated. For Gomulka it appears as the crowning success of his life's work—and that not only in the light of his fall two weeks later. On the evening of the day the treaty was signed Cyrankiewicz declared that 7 December 1970 would perhaps come to be seen as an historic date, one which might outweigh 1 September 1939 (when Hitler attacked Poland). Gomulka's successor, Gierek, wants to continue the policy of normalizing relations with the Federal Republic. His very first statements leave no doubt about this.

Nevertheless the Federal Republic will still be a security problem for Poland in the future. The Warsaw treaty still has to be ratified, and this is bound up with ratification of the Moscow treaty, and thus indirectly with the negotiations on Berlin as well. This dependence upon the world political situation and the question of whether the Brandt Government, with its frail parliamentary majority, will be strong enough to get the treaties through the *Bundestag*, give cause enough for doubt. But even if the treaties come into force the West German scene, in Polish eyes, remains so unpredictable that doubt, caution and vigilance are felt to be needed. Brandt's advantage in the negotiations, his personal stock of trustworthiness, is at the same time the weak point of the Federal Republic. The desired 'normalization' between Poland and West Germany can only become a reality, in the Polish view, when it rests on firmer foundations than the 'accident' of a well-disposed government in Bonn. As a member of the *Sejm* put it at the end of 1970, there is need for a 'ratification by the people'. He did not mean by this a plebiscite but a positive attitude on the part of the public, and co-operation from all social forces in the Federal Republic.

In Warsaw's view nationalist impulses in West Germany have been

[24] *Tribuna Ludu*, 2 June 1969.

weakened. Connoisseurs of the situation in Bonn, and the Polish press, note differences within the CDU. And even the idea that a subsequent conservative government could only with difficulty go back on the position taken up by Brandt and Scheel is gaining ground. Nevertheless a remnant of insecurity remains. Anxieties have been substantially reduced by the Warsaw treaty, but they have not vanished. The treaty has given rise to hope that a new relationship of collaboration will be attainable, but there is as yet no certainty of this. Distrust is too deep-rooted to be removed by a treaty.

Dangers from West Germany

The Warsaw leadership, at least in recent years, have not taken the view that a war was intended, or perhaps even being prepared for, in the Federal Republic. If the account of Gomulka's former interpreter, Erwin Weit, is to be trusted, Gomulka described statements of this kind by Ulbricht as 'nonsense', and explained them by reference to the difficult position of the SED, for which one had to have understanding.[25] At the last Polish Party Congress in November 1968 the Party leaders described the dangers from Bonn in the same way as he saw the danger of war as such. He did not say that the Federal Republic was working for war, but that 'its whole previous history is full of actions directed against peace'. A great many statements, both public and private, indicate that this is the prevailing opinion in the country. In the summer of 1964, at the Fourth Party Congress, Gomulka was still speaking exclusively of 'militaristic circles' which, like similar circles in America, had not given up the idea of a 'hot' war. But three years later he explicitly pointed to the 'cold' war as the policy with which Bonn was trying to attain its objectives. At the Fifth Party Congress in November 1968 the Polish Party leader said that all governments of the Federal Republic, right up to the Grand Coalition of Kiesinger and Brandt, were 'guided by a programme that provides . . . for the alteration of national frontiers in Europe, the liquidation of the German Democratic Republic, and the rebuilding of a militaristic Greater Germany within the frontiers of 1937'. However, the next two sentences should be read carefully: '*At bottom,* this is a programme of aggression. Any attempt to carry it out would bring with it the outbreak of war.' Thus Gomulka leaves open the question whether Bonn is determined to put into practice its alleged programme despite the risk of war.

A paragraph further on it becomes clear that he does not credit any West German Government with plans for war. Their hope has been 'to compel . . . the Soviet Union to agree to the so-called unification of Germany . . . with the help of the aggressive NATO bloc'. This is Adenauer's 'policy of strength' which, as is well known, was always a

[25] Erwin Weit, *Ostblock intern*, Hamburg 1970, pp. 138–9.

policy of negotiation, but supported by military strength. The Polish Party leader ascribed to the Kiesinger–Brandt Government a new political tactic, namely to break up the unity of the Socialist states and isolate the GDR in order to be able eventually to 'liquidate' it. Gomulka's view became quite clear in the summer of 1969. On the one hand, he declared, the policy of certain West German circles concealed a 'potential danger of war'. On the other, however, 'military conflicts in Europe are simply unthinkable in our time'.[26] At the Moscow Party Conference in June 1969 he expressed the opinion that the balance of forces had 'destroyed imperialism's hopes of overcoming Socialism in individual countries by classical armed counterrevolution supported by external intervention'. For this reason the 'imperialist strategists laid the main emphasis on the struggle to undermine Socialism by ideological and political subversion'. The Polish Party leader's judgment was thus identical with his East German colleague's—the danger was political, ideological and economic, not, or only in the very last analysis, military.

This is not to say that the danger has become less. As the old fear of the 'expellee' organizations and the 'militarists' has died away, there developed, in the eyes of many Poles, a new threat which is not yet acute but could become so in the foreseeable future. The best exposition of this view is given in a passage by Ryszard Wojna: 'The essence of the German danger to Poland is different today from what it was 30, 50 or 100 years ago. Above all our frontier is now with one of two German states which is our ally and, like Poland, belongs to a military system which, in practice, leaves German militarism no opportunity for revenge.'[27] The writer then specifies and justifies the Polish demands that Bonn recognize Poland's Western frontier and the existence of the GDR, renounce access to atomic weapons and so on, on the grounds that a lasting peace in Europe is only possible on the basis of the *status quo*. Wojna goes on to say that

> The problem does not end here, however. The economic potential of the German Federal Republic has already reached such a level of development that all the variants of Bonn policy currently being aired on the Rhine come down, in more or less disguised form, to the same thing—the creation of a 'Greater Germany', even if under the cloak of West European integration. For this reason the nature of the German danger has to be assessed and recognized over the long term. Concentration on the survival of neo-Nazism in the Federal Republic is not enough to prepare our society against the complex and special nature of this danger.

[26] At the ceremonial meeting of the *Sejm* on the occasion of the twenty-fifth anniversary of the Polish Peoples' Republic, 21 July 1969.
[27] *Zycie Warszawy*, 23 March 1969.

Polish policy towards the German problem will preserve a continuity that will not cease with the death of the last Nazi or the last former inmate of Auschwitz.

Thus the increasing power of the Federal Republic gives rise to new fears for the future. It is inconceivable in Warsaw that the 'economic giant' will remain a 'political dwarf', especially as it maintains the strongest army in Western Europe. West Germany's growing influence in the EEC and NATO, which is already detectable, could with the passage of time become a hegemony over Western Europe. In the atomic field the same process could lead from joint to main control by Bonn over a West European nuclear force. As early as 1964 Gomulka warned against the Federal Republic's aspirations to great-power status backed by nuclear weapons. It is hardly possible to overestimate Poland's fear of a German state capable of backing up its policy with weapons of mass destruction. There are, it is true, two factors contributing substantial reassurance—first, the signature of the nuclear Non-Proliferation Treaty by the Brandt–Scheel Government, and second, the realization that the West Europeans are scarcely less opposed to an increase in Bonn's nuclear power than the East Europeans. But quite apart from the Federal Republic's nuclear status there is in Warsaw's view reason for disquiet, though from a very different direction.

The heart of all these anxieties is a West Germany strengthened by Western Europe. For many Poles it seems an almost logical consequence of their view of West Germany that Bonn, if it can obtain a broader basis of support, will pursue the kind of policy urged by Franz-Josef Strauss and, in a more moderate form, by others also. The failure of this policy is as much feared as its success. Thus Warsaw directs its polemics against Strauss not only out of fear lest his design succeed and the Eastern system of alliances be dissolved and transferred, bit by bit, to the West. A more immediate and urgent consideration is that a powerful concentration of force in Western Europe will evoke, not co-operation between the two parts of the continent, but confrontation. It is not only softening up that is feared, but also, and at least as much, a hardening up within the Warsaw Pact in order to impede this process. Strauss's 'Grand Design' for Europe, so one hears in Warsaw in many versions, is a policy according to the spirit that led Europe into the cold war and allowed the Iron Curtain to develop. Its result would be, not to supersede the military blocs but to reinforce them and that would mean, ultimately, an increased danger of war, or at least a reduced prospect of a firmly based peace.

But this of course is only the security aspect. It is equally important, and for most Poles probably seems even more important, that Strauss (who is regarded as the spokesman and symbol of a whole trend) recommends co-operation of a kind and in a manner that would not make easier the sort of co-operation the Poles urgently want, but more difficult or even impossible. A man who proclaims as the object of his policy the strengthening of his own alliance and the dissolution of his opponents', cannot expect the opposing camp to assure him of its eagerness to co-operate.

Dangers from a United Germany

In the Polish view this policy is a threat above all to the GDR. As Gomulka puts it, the 'liquidation' of the GDR is the 'greatest strategic objective of the West German bourgeoisie'. But Poland's fate seems to be indissolubly bound up with the existence of East Germany. 'Our Party and the Government of People's Poland have always regarded the security and sovereignty of the GDR and the inviolability of her frontiers as equivalent to the security and inviolability of the frontiers of Poland'. This declaration by Gomulka at the Seventh SED Party Congress has been endorsed by most politicians in authority in Poland. At any rate those of an age to remember Hitler are largely convinced that an 'annexation' of East Germany would form simply the first stage in a renewed 'Drive to the East'. A Western Germany reaching out as far as the Oder–Neisse seems to them intolerable, even though it were solemnly to endorse this frontier. Once the Germans start to expand, nothing stops them except military force. Hitler too proceeded step by step. So long as he was still busy with one victim, he guaranteed the rights of the next.

But even if one leaves out of account the more than understandable traumatic experiences of the generation of whom in some cases half or three-quarters were exterminated, there remains a lively Polish interest in the GDR. The main reasons have been openly stated by Polish leaders. Thus Jan Szydlak, Central Committee Secretary and Politburo candidate, said on 5 September 1969: 'The rise of the GDR has substantially restricted German militarism in geopolitical terms, pushed it back to the West of the Elbe and greatly reduced its material and human strength.'[28] If one adds to this Cyrankiewicz's remark that for the first time Poland's frontier was with a peaceful German state, an ally,[29] it follows that the situation could not be more favourable for Poland:

(1) The existence of a Socialist East Germany weakens Germany's potential by division.

(2) The GDR forms a barrier[30] against the stronger, ideologically differently orientated, and therefore more dangerous part of Germany.

[28] *PAP Daily News*, 6 September 1969.
[29] In a speech in Krakow, 23 May 1959.
[30] The term 'barrier' is used in the speeches of both Gomulka at the Karlovy Vary Conference of Communist parties and Kliszko at the Eighth Plenary of the Central Committee on 17 May 1967.

(3) Poland is allied with, and in the same ideological camp as, the weaker and therefore less dangerous part of Germany.

Any change in this situation would be bound to reduce Poland's security. A reunified Germany on the Western model would destroy the East–West balance and threaten to alter the relationship of forces to the disadvantage of the East. Given that the Poles—and not only they—are already afraid of a West German dominance in Western Europe, the hegemony of a united Germany over the Western part of the continent would be inevitable, even if the most saintly of men were to rule in Bonn or Berlin.

Considerations along these lines do not apply only to the improbable event of a Western-orientated reunion of Germany. There could be an understanding between the two German states which Poland would regard no longer as merely useful for *détente*, but as dubious for herself. In 1969 there were already complaints that the GDR was building up trade with West Germany, bringing in foreign currency as its own privilege, and thus safeguarding its indirect connection with the EEC, while in the East its only serious effort was directed towards integration with the Soviet Union. The anxiety of some Poles lest their country remain semi-agricultural among highly industrialized neighbour states does not rank as a security problem. None the less one already meets people in Warsaw who find more nationalistic features in East than in West Germany. Above all, however, the GDR is economically stronger than Poland (as is very well known there). If it were to enter into close economic co-operation with the Federal Republic, or if the German confederation once urged by East Berlin were to come about, this would be bound very soon to arouse the old Polish fear of joint domination by their German and Russian neighbours.

In the most improbable event of Germany being united on the SED pattern, this fear would reach its highest pitch—probably higher than if reunification occurred under Bonn's aegis. Threatening as a 'Western' united Germany would appear, this would be so not only in Warsaw but also in Moscow, whence the Poles could hope for reasonably certain support. But the position would be really black if they could no longer rely on mutual Russo-German opposition on grounds of ideology and international politics. A united Germany in ideological and political agreement with the Soviet Union and perhaps even militarily allied with it would bring Poland into the same fatal situation that several times in recent centuries has cost its very existence as a state. To avoid this has been the basic principle of Polish policy since 1945. On this point the clarity of statements from Warsaw leaves nothing to be desired: '75 million Germans, 230 million Russians—what would happen to the 30 million Poles in between?' and 'A united Socialist Germany?—we are not going to commit suicide!'

Poland's security requirements thus demand the maintenance of

Germany in its present condition. It has sometimes been assumed that
it was in Poland's interest to acquire an immediate territorial contact
with the West. According to this view a Western unification of Germany
would be desirable for Warsaw, so long as the Oder–Neisse frontier
was guaranteed. But it is not only the security considerations already
mentioned that tell against this theory, considerations that would
apply to any regime in Warsaw for the foreseeable future. There is
also the question whether a common frontier with the West is an
advantage at all for a state in the Soviet sphere looking for more
internal or external independence. The experience available points
to an important distinction. A country that leaves the alliance, like
Yugoslavia or Albania, should not be enclosed by Soviet or Soviet-
allied territory. But a country that is neither willing nor able to leave
the alliance—and both these points, or at least the second, certainly
apply to Poland—is probably in a better position to follow its own way
and its own national interests if it does not border on NATO, as
Czechoslovakia does. The prospect of the Kremlin tolerating independent behaviour is greater for a country like Rumania whose
geographical situation hardly permits a separation from the Soviet
alliance system. Thus there is some reason to believe that Khrushchev
tolerated the 'Polish October' because East Germany, allied to and
occupied by the Soviet Union, provided a barrier between this development and the West. In this paradoxical way the GDR supplies Poland
with a shield that might seem as useful to future Polish governments
as it was to Gomulka in 1956.

Relations with the Soviet Union

Any consideration of Poland's security requirements brings out a
vital distinction: while the Western frontier was in question, at least
until the end of the 1960s, the Eastern frontier has been unchallenged
since 1945. Poland certainly has no prospect of regaining the territories
lost to the Soviet Union in 1939, for Moscow retains what it has gained.
But it has no intention of gaining any more. So the Polish Eastern
frontier is secure. At the same time the Kremlin has provided Poland
with a replacement in the West for its losses in the East and has
guaranteed these gains. Thus the Western frontier has also been
secured, thanks to the Soviet Union. Poland owes the content of its
territory—the 'most advantageous for the nation'[31]—to its Eastern
neighbour, and this will continue to be the case for as long as a desire
for frontier changes may exist or reappear in the West.

The closeness of the relationship between Warsaw and Moscow
depends partly upon the extent of Poland's fear of West Germany. If,
as a result of the Warsaw treaty, normal relations develop and are

[31] *Zycie Warszawy* (see footnote [1]).

gradually expanded into broader collaboration, this is bound to have effects on Warsaw's relations with Moscow. The more secure the Western frontier seems to be, the less becomes Polish dependence on the Soviet guarantee. In the long term the dangers for Poland may change in order of priority—the West Germans moving into second place, the Russians into first. Even before the conclusion of the Warsaw treaty it was said in Poland that the Soviet alliance was not a love match but a marriage of convenience. The reasons of convenience remain very strong, even independently of relations with Bonn, but resentment against Poland's giant neighbour is not negligible either. And whereas the German danger is becoming theoretical for the generation that did not experience the war and the occupation, the presence of the Russians, although they keep their soldiers practically hidden away, is concrete and immediate.

In addition there is a certain change of mood in regard to the past. Less emphasis is put on the sufferings of the Poles during the war, more on their deeds. If this development is maintained, as is probable, it could lead to a diminished fear of Germany. On the other hand it is well known that throughout Eastern Europe self-confidence and independence *vis-à-vis* the Soviet Union are conditioned by the extent to which a country contributed to its own liberation from the Germans. Tito provides the textbook example, but Gomulka too showed himself anxious during the war to achieve the greatest possible 'self-help', while Soviet interests lay in the opposite direction.[32] Characteristic of the present attitude in Poland is a statement by the Deputy Defence Minister and head of the political administration of the Polish People's Army. Poland, said General Urbanowicz in the summer of 1969, had carried on 'the war to its victorious conclusion for longer than all other countries' and had made a 'precisely calculable contribution to the destruction of German fascism' . . . Poland, a small country terribly ravaged by the war, ranks immediately behind the great powers in its military contribution.'[33]

Poland's national self-awareness created something of a special position for her, the largest of the Soviet Union's allies, even in Stalin's time, and especially afterwards. In 1948 this cost a man like Gomulka, who in his last years seemed to be a 'fanatic for unity',[34] his power and put him into prison for 'nationalistic right wing deviation' and the desire for equal rights with the Soviet Union. But the real crisis point in Soviet–Polish relations came in 1956. Since then Warsaw has had to take into account a latent but constant danger from Moscow. The dramatic days of the 'Polish October' prove that the 'radical turning point' in relations between the two neighbouring states was by no

[32] Hansjakob Stehle, *op. cit.*, p. 47.
[33] In an article published in *Neues Deutschland*, 19 July 1969.
[34] Angela Nacken, *Frankfurter Allgemeine Zeitung*, 30 May 1969.

means as radical as is asserted in the text of the mutual assistance treaty eight and a half years later.

When Khrushchev, Mikoyan, Molotov and Kaganovich flew unannounced to Warsaw to prevent Gomulka's re-election, this was more than mere interference in Poland's internal affairs. It was the Stalinistic claim to take the allies' major decisions for them. The Poles for a time refused their unwelcome guests permission to enter, and backed up the right to choose their own leadership with the threat of military resistance to the Soviet troops. They went to the brink of war to defend their independence. But both sides in the confrontation kept their heads and this prevented the worst from happening. The relatively good relations that subsequently grew up between the two were made possible because they had learned the lessons of the collision they so narrowly avoided.

The Soviet leadership took note of Gomulka's words: 'No nation in the world is so sensitive about its independence and sovereignty as Poland.'[35] The Kremlin has paid heed to this sensitivity, and relations between Warsaw and Moscow have become normal to the extent that Poland enjoys a relative independence. The Poles for their part, as one observer with many years' experience put it, became realistic after 1956 for the first time in their history. They took note in their turn that their independence could only be relative—'Absolute autarchy and sovereignty are an anachronism.'

Poland does not have an acute security problem in regard to the Soviet Union. But after the experiences of October 1956 future difficulties cannot be ruled out. The first of these is summed up in the word 'Rapallo': the second is the threat of the fate Poland so narrowly escaped in October 1956, and Czechoslovakia suffered on 21 August 1968.

'Rapallo' Fears

Good relations between Moscow and Bonn are in fact welcomed in Warsaw from one point of view, because they promote *détente*. On the other hand, they are also viewed with concern similar to that felt in East Berlin, especially as the Kremlin does not seem to be very communicative towards its much smaller ally. Quite apart from historically based fears which are gradually fading away, a German–Soviet relationship is especially easy to imagine in Warsaw if West German strength meets with weakness in Eastern Europe. This is not the least of the reasons why the Polish leadership looks with concern upon all developments that could damage the solidarity of the Warsaw Pact or involve Moscow too deeply in conflict with China. At least since the widely publicized clash on the Ussuri River early in 1969 the same anxiety is to be met with in certain East European capitals that

[35] Quoted in Stehle, *op. cit.*, p. 54.

affected some West European politicians at the height of the Vietnam war—anxiety lest their guardian and patron enter too deeply into Asian affairs and become too casual or yielding on the European front for its allies' security. Like Moscow and East Berlin, Warsaw looks on any hint of a *rapprochement* between Peking on the one side, and Bonn or Washington on the other, with mistrust and with speculations that often go far beyond the intention or capacity of the parties themselves.

But how in fact could the Russians and Germans join together at the expense of the Poles? A change in the Oder–Neisse frontier is not in the Soviet interest. If it were in favour of Western Germany the Soviet Union would irretrievably weaken its strategic forward area in Poland, both politically and morally. Above all Moscow would lose all credibility as leader and guarantor of Socialism. But the Kremlin could not agree to a frontier revision, even in favour of the GDR or a united Socialist Germany, because as soon as one starts revising anywhere, the way is opened to all the other revisionist demands— between Poland and Czechoslovakia, Hungary and Rumania, Bulgaria and Yugoslavia, and eventually the Soviet Union itself would have to reckon with claims—from Poland, Slovakia and Rumania. If only to keep the peace in its own camp Moscow dare not touch the *status quo* anywhere within its sphere of influence. But of course to leave an ultimate grain of uncertainty is part of the classical method of domination—especially effective where, as with Poland, there is an historically based feeling of insecurity. However, such a threat cannot be kept up, in the long run, by a pure fiction. The fact that there are fears in Warsaw about the external position is largely accounted for by the existence of internal fears.

Ideological Weaknesses

Almost all the fears of the Polish leaders in relation to the Soviet Union and Germany can only be fully understood if the ideological dangers are taken into account. Poland, like nearly all the Pact countries, is vulnerable to three things: nationalism, Western living standards, and Western democratic freedoms, both for individuals and in the organization of political life.[36] Foreign observers speak of a 'deeply disturbed relationship to the state, to all authority'.—'Everything that comes down from above must be smashed, sabotaged, at whatever cost and however reasonable it is!' The Poles are even harder to

[36] 'Revisionism', Gomulka told the Fifth Party Congress in 1969, 'draws its support from the pockets of former bourgeois modes of thought among various groups of the population . . . This heritage is expressed in certain circles in vestiges of nationalism, in servility towards the West and in a bourgeois style of life, in egoism and self-seeking, in striving to "get on" at the expense of society, in an anarchistic attitude to state power and in lack of social and civil discipline.'

educate in Socialism than other peoples—though they have perhaps, as a thoughtful observer in Warsaw said, become more Socialist than they realize in the course of two decades.

In 1967 Politburo member Kliszko[37] produced a list of the difficulties the Party leadership had to contend with. He felt that the Poles were learning enough, and the right things, about the West German 'militarists' and Vietnam, from the national press, radio and television. Otherwise, however, what they heard and read about the West told them more about new models of cars and the Beatles than about the hard living conditions of the working class in capitalist countries. Too little was done to counteract bourgeois propaganda which was trying to hypnotize the Poles with the ideal of a consumer society and at the same time campaign against the leading role of the Communist party, under the slogan of 'freedom', democracy, a free play of political forces, and civil rights. Too little action was taken against 'provincial nationalism' in relation to Socialist neighbouring states, and too little for positive explanation of their life and development. Finally, too little was said about the Socialist attitude to work.

There is nothing surprising in Kliszko seeing the internal and external enemies of Socialism as closely linked, or in his polemics against American 'bridge-building', West German *Ostpolitik*, ideological coexistence and the 'reactionary sections of the Church hierarchy'. But his account of the sharpening class struggle does seem remarkable: the experience of recent years has clearly proved that increasing *détente*, direct contacts, stimulation of scientific and cultural exchanges, and the tourist trade have not diminished the struggle between bourgeois and Socialist ideology in the slightest. 'On the contrary all this has, in a certain sense, even strengthened it.'

One of the main problems, as everywhere, is the young people, perhaps still more so in Poland which is a specially 'young' country. Kliszko thinks it is becoming 'more important every year' to disseminate the right principles and views, because half the population have begun their conscious lives in Peoples' Poland and cannot appreciate the difference from what went on before. The Party leadership's idea of what needs to be put across shows what is lacking. Thus the young people underestimate two things—the advantages they are offered by Socialist conditions, and the dangers that come from national and class enemies, especially the West Germans. The new generation is little inclined to follow 'the old lines of political orthodoxy and ideological dogma', they would rather be a 'generation of coexistence' than, as Kliszko hopes, a 'generation of struggle'.

The indifference of young people to the experiences, achievements and therefore the basic principles of the older is a problem for all Socialist countries—and not for these alone. It seems to be specific

[37] *Op. cit.*, (footnote [30]).

to Poland that there is more marked anxiety there that the new generation will not pay enough heed to the lessons of World War II. Some
Poles even take this as a reason why it is necessary to establish European security as quickly and firmly as possible. The young people
must be given a Europe in which peace is guaranteed.

Three Cases of Ideological Danger

What form could the ideological danger take for Poland? In somewhat
schematized form one can think of three cases:

(1) A strong liberal or even democratic trend in Poland.
(2) A strong national trend in Poland, leading to an autonomous
   foreign policy.
(3) A strong democratic and national trend in another Socialist
   country, threatening to 'infect' Poland, and destroy the unity
   of the Warsaw Pact.

Poland lived through the first case after October 1956. The freedoms
that then emerged of their own accord rather than being granted were
cut down by Gomulka in the following period, gradually but systematically, to a level that no longer endangers the authoritarian (not
totalitarian) character of the regime. Even the student demonstrations
of March 1968 seemed to the Party leadership a threat against which
they defended themselves with the ruthlessness of fear. The danger
they believed they were facing then was the same that they recognized
in the Prague reform movement:[38] a creeping, almost unnoticeable
process of inner relaxation, which would lead to a growing outer link
with the West. This connection between domestic and foreign policy
is one of the basic convictions of the Polish leadership, most vividly
expressed by Gomulka as early as 1956: 'Only a Socialist Poland can
be free and sovereign.'[39]

The conclusion from this sentence is clear. An uncontrolled democratic development that soon got out of hand would begin by endanger-
ing the regime and Leninist-type Socialism, and go on to threaten the

[38] The Polish Major-General Czalpa declared later, in justification of 21
August 1968, that 'certain similarities' could be seen between the 'backward
looking forces' in Czechoslovakia and those who inspired the 'March events'
in Poland: 'The glorification of the same slogans of "renewal", used in a
pseudo-national and "democratic" tone, was common to both. There was a
convergence of goals. There was the misuse of declarations about "freedom and
pure Socialism" so as to water down their class content . . . in order to cut back
the leading role of the Party, to isolate the Party from the life of the people, to
reduce the future prospects of Socialism and thereupon to destroy it . . . The
banner of "Improving Socialism" has lately become the main solution proposed in revisionist and nationalist circles. This banner was unfurled in
Prague in the same way as in Warsaw in March.' (Quoted in Andreas Fischer,
Was bleibt vom Prager Frühling? Hamburg: Rissener Studien, 1969.)
[39] Quoted in Stehle, *op. cit.*, p. 56.

security of the country. Poland would lose its unconditional Soviet support, would fall into a certain dependence on the West and once more become a pawn in the foreign policy of larger powers—or, what is much more probable, become the victim of a new 21 August.

The second scenario starts with Polish nationalism, which seems to be independent of generations, and continues to be a source of great anxiety to realistic leaders in Warsaw. Prime Minister Cyrankiewicz explained to the Czechs (in an interview with *Rude Pravo* on 11 June 1969) the dangers of a country going-it-alone. No single Socialist country, he maintained, could become in its own right an 'effective counter-weight to imperialist aggressiveness'. For 'we only count if we act together with the Soviet Union. Without the Soviet Union we should be powerless . . . Any illusions existing in this field can only lead to the isolation of an individual Socialist country, and isolation is always an invitation to aggression, not always military but often political.'

Nationalism, however, in the Polish leaders' view contains dangers not only to the West, but also to the East: 'In Poland nationalism may start out under this or that aspect, but in its ultimate effect it will always show its anti-Soviet claws.'[40] Behind this statement of Politburo member Jedrychowski lies the fear that the Poles might be led by their traditional recklessness to upset the balance painfully constructed in 1956 between relative independence for Warsaw and limited influence for Moscow.

Much more imminent, however, is a strongly 'national' policy, moderated by tactical considerations, rather on the lines followed by Ceausescu. There is a great deal of unspoken admiration for the Rumanian head of state, and the polemics of the Warsaw press against Bucharest in 1968 show that the Rumanian attitude is taken as an example by many Poles.

Thoughtful Poles, however, point to important differences between their country and Rumania. They consider that for Warsaw a foreign policy *à la* Bucharest would be either impossible or much more risky, for two reasons:

(1) The threshold of Soviet tolerance is substantially lower for Poland, because it is more important to Moscow strategically and politically.

(2) In Poland foreign policy departures on the Rumanian scale would be accompanied by growing internal demands from the population and Party. A forced independence in foreign relations would have the effect of encouraging and justifying more independent, i.e. more liberal and democratic conditions within the country. What Ceausescu can still keep under control and canalize through careful internal reforms, owing to the lesser degree of development in Rumania, might become a flood difficult to stem in Poland, and likewise in Czecho-

[40] Quoted in Ludwig Zimmerer, *Die Zeit*, 19 July 1968.

slovakia, Hungary, and indeed the GDR as well. But Moscow would hardly tolerate both external and internal independence. The culmination of a sharply national foreign policy would mean for Poland too the danger of a 21 August.

The third case of ideological danger occurred in 1968. In so far as Warsaw imagined the development of its southern neighbours on the lines of a Yugoslavia (internally and externally) or Finland, three conclusions followed for concerned Poles:

(a) Political infection comes about essentially through the effect of example, especially when it appears as relevant. When Albania left the Eastern alliance, first *de facto* and then formally, all Pact members could put up with this without difficulty, owing to the remoteness and insignificance of the country. The same development in Prague, but above all the establishment of a democracy in part in West European form, would have an importance as a symbol and example that can scarcely be exaggerated. It would prove that a member of the Warsaw Pact can escape from Soviet hegemony (even though it remained in a Finland-like status), and above all that a Leninist form of Socialism is reversible. The moral effect of such an example on all, especially the neighbouring Socialist countries, would be extraordinary. No doubt few believe that this sort of Socialism will prevail throughout the whole world. But that it will endure where it now exists is one of the permanent and inalienable convictions on which the rule of all Communist parties is based. Proof that there existed, internally as well as externally, not merely relaxations within a rigid framework but a real alternative, could bring most East European regimes under mortal pressure from the people, and to some extent from the parties as well. This would certainly be the case for Poland.

(b) Czechoslovakia's territory and its fourteen divisions would be lost for the defence of the Warsaw Pact. A change of alliances or even the stationing of NATO units in Czechoslovakia would, it is true, be beyond any realistic consideration. Nevertheless there would still be a weakening of the Eastern alliance, which would affect Poland especially, since it would no longer have a firm ally on its long southern frontier, but instead a 'soft' neutral. No general, and no politician either, looks on such a possibility without anxiety, even if he believes in a nuclear balance of forces that would give Poland reliable protection against military attack even after a defection by Czechoslovakia.

(c) The decisive factor, however, was probably that Czechoslovakia borders on the Federal Republic. The key to understanding Poland's decision to take part in the occupation lies in the 'attitude and policy of the Federal Republic'. Other matters can be left aside. Even if this interpretation, given in a Polish newspaper,[41] is exaggerated, the

[41] *Glos Pracy*, 26 August 1968 (quoted in Harald Laeuen, *Osteuropa*, October/November 1968).

importance of the German danger is shown by the very fact that in 1968 it could be put forward in Warsaw as reason and justification for a policy which was as contrary to Polish traditions as it was to Gomulka's own principles—namely that the Polish freedom fighters of the past fought 'for our freedom and yours'. For Gomulka the independence of each Communist Party, at least in internal policy, was always a guide-line for action. It does seem that so far as the occupation of Czechoslovakia was concerned, the gap between leadership and people was smaller in Poland than in any other of the occupying states (except perhaps the Soviet Union). The conjuring up of a 'new Munich' and a repetition of the development that led to September 1939[42] has brought about in the broad mass of the population, so far as one can judge without actual figures, not approval but a certain understanding for the use of force against a neighbouring state[43] that in Poland is regarded as unreliable anyway.

What many Poles seemed to fear was not merely a neutral or unconcerned Prague but a Czechoslovakia which, by reason of this neutrality and unconcern, would come under West German influence, first economically and then by slow degrees politically as well:

> Bonn's intention before 21 August consisted in dividing developments in Czechoslovakia into stages, intended to cover a longer period. The objective was to prepare the Soviet Union and the other Socialist countries, slowly and gradually, for changes in relations between the German Federal Republic and Czechoslovakia. But these tactics were spoiled by the impatience of the anti-Socialist forces in Czechoslovakia.[44]

In the Polish view the gradual extension of the Federal Republic's influence over the whole of Eastern Europe West of the Bug was Bonn's main goal. After a breakthrough in Czechoslovakia the next to feel the pull of West Germany would be the GDR, followed or accompanied by Poland itself. The results would extend on the one hand from stricter Pact discipline and intensified East–West confrontation to measures like those of 21 August, and on the other from inner softening up within and around Poland through to 'Rapallo' deals that would further cut down Warsaw's room for manœuvre. The possible threat of such developments in the future would increase, in Polish eyes, in direct proportion to the increasing strength of the Federal Republic in Western Europe, and the increasing preoccupation of the Soviet Union with China.

The clinching argument, always used in Warsaw on subsequent occasions in support of 21 August, runs as follows: Developments in

---

[42] Cyrankiewicz, 31 August 1968.   [43] Cf. *The Times*, 20 May 1969, p. 9.
[44] Report in the weekly *Kierunki* of a discussion among leading Warsaw journalists and collaborators of the Institute for International Affairs.

Czechoslovakia gave rise to fears of change in the East–West balance. This anxiety can only be understood if one takes into account first and foremost the political considerations: a strategic weakening of the Eastern side, leading ultimately to fears of military pressure or even action by the West, seems conceivable purely as the result of political weakness. In Polish eyes only a country or alliance that has been 'softened up' is vulnerable to pressure.

III. SECURITY POLICY AND PROSPECTS

The Alliance

Poland is as convinced as the GDR that the Federal Republic is the main danger, and the Polish idea of security is therefore similar to that of East Berlin, at least in its basic features. Security policy takes the Soviet alliance as its immovable basis and the unity of the Socialist camp seems indispensable to it. Just as the SED is anxious to build up the position of East Germany as a state in its own right, so the Polish regime has done all it could right from the start to integrate the former German Eastern provinces as an inseparable part of the unity of the Polish state. In both cases the power of the *fait accompli* is being used in the service of security policy.

But apart from this agreement of principle, there are differences. The most important is that Warsaw does everything in a less one-sided way and with lesser and varying intensity. There is however a difference in attitude to the Soviet Union. Even for Warsaw the Soviet alliance means in the first place protection against the West. The best possible relations with Moscow are maintained in order to strengthen Polish influence there, so that Poland's great ally does not neglect Polish interests, either inside or outside the Socialist camp. At the same time these relations are cultivated to avoid dangerous situations like that of October 1956. Of course it is vitally important to all the Warsaw Pact regimes to retain the confidence of Moscow. But in Poland, where matters have twice come close to the stage of armed conflict, attention to Moscow and suppression of anti-Soviet feeling in the country are basic needs of security policy.

As in the GDR, and other Socialist states too, the link with Moscow matters ultimately because it gives the ruling party leadership backing at home. This has not always been the case and need not always remain so. In 1956 Gomulka came to power *against* the Soviet Union. But by the end of his career he stood to a large extent *with* the Soviet Union. The more the party leader is compelled to strike a balance between rival forces and groups in the country instead of subduing them, the more he is inclined and obliged, in order to strengthen his own position, to seek the support of the Kremlin and to avoid any strain in relations with Moscow.

A similar development can be seen in the Polish attitude to the principle of preserving the unity of the Socialist camp. So long as it has been a question of unified defence against a supposedly aggressive Western policy, of recognition of Poland's western frontier and the security of the GDR, Warsaw has always set the highest value on unity. Poland also has an economic interest in close co-operation within COMECON. But where the unity of internal policy in the Socialist countries has been in question, the Polish leadership has changed its attitude. After 1956 Gomulka was the first and the most resolute in fighting for a national way to Socialism. He disapproved, though cautiously, of the Soviet intervention in Hungary and the execution of Imre Nagy in 1958. But when Czechoslovakia was occupied in 1968, he took an active part, and barely three months later expressed himself at the Polish Party Congress in terms scarcely different from the so-called Brezhnev doctrine.[45] In the summer of 1969 Gomulka, back from the conference of Communist Parties in Moscow, launched a polemic against the Italian Communists and against Ceausescu, who had put forward the idea that 'the proletariat and Communist Parties take as the basis for developing their political line the particular circumstances and conditions in which they work'. The Polish Party leader explained that, on the contrary, particular circumstances could account for

> only some of the differences in the attitudes of Communist Parties —above all differences in connection with the methods of the struggle for Socialism in a particular country. National peculiarities cannot excuse differences in political line which lead to a falling away from the basic principles of Marxism–Leninism and proletarian internationalism and which bring a party or group of parties into opposition to the whole Communist movement and thus sow the seeds of a split.

After an attack on nationalism, 'the ideological cause of centrifugal and splitting tendencies', comes this remarkable statement: 'In some of the European People's Democracies revisionism is characterized by anti-Soviet nationalism and cosmopolitanism in its attitude towards the capitalist West.'[46] This open attack on Warsaw Pact allies, certainly including Rumania, showed what Gomulka feared and was

[45] 'Every Communist and worker's party is responsible to its own working class and to its own people; it represents the interests and aims of its country and decides by itself the line of policy. But these interests and aims cannnot be dealt with in isolation and much less in opposition to the interests, aims and goals of Socialism in the international context. No difference in view on the tactics of the fight and the methods of building Socialism can justify the behaviour of those parties which avoid this international responsibility and take the road of nationalism.'

[46] At the Plenary of the Central Committee, 25 June 1969.

trying to combat in his own country. The opposition with which he had to contend was predominantly national in tendency, and the Czechoslovak development in 1968 was an inspiration to all liberal-minded people who wanted a wider opening to the West. To Gomulka it seemed necessary to hold both tendencies in check, and not simply for the sake of his own position. The grand old man of Polish politics wanted above all to protect from themselves his Polish people — restless, emotional, freedom-loving sometimes to the point of anarchy, and utterly non-Communist as they are. And so he, who was once regarded (for the most part unjustly) as a nationalist, revisionist and opponent of Moscow, had become the steadfast advocate of a policy aimed at close ties with the Soviet Union and strict discipline within the Warsaw Pact, and marked by great caution towards the West.

Of course it would be an over-simplification to explain this transformation solely in terms of changes in Polish domestic politics. Europe at the end of the 1950s looked very different from Europe in the middle of the 1960s, when Polish foreign policy merged almost completely with that of Moscow and East Berlin. After 1956 people in Warsaw did not yet seem to have regarded the division of Germany as final. Thus Poland could not entirely rely on the GDR as a protective barrier. On the other hand less attention needed to be paid to East Berlin's interests. But to reach an arrangement with the Federal Republic, which at that time still had no atomic weapons and carried less political weight, seemed both necessary and possible. In the following period both German states became stronger. The GDR demanded more consideration and offered more security, and Warsaw and East Berlin moved closer to each other ideologically. West Germany however, in Polish eyes, became more dangerous as it grew stronger. This suggested to the Poles that they should base their security above all on a close connection between Moscow, Warsaw and East Berlin. And invocation of the supposed dangers of West German *revanchism* proved useful for uniting the people behind their leaders at a time of internal political tension.

Finally, an important factor in the more markedly Eastward orientation of Polish policy has been deep disappointment that, despite efforts of many kinds, all attempts to conclude agreements with the West on European security have foundered — above all, as people see it in Warsaw (to a large extent rightly) against the rigid posture of the Federal Republic.

Proposals on European Security

Poland's plans for European security distinguish Warsaw's security policy from that of all Moscow's other allies. Poland was the first of the Pact countries to concern itself with its own foreign policy — within the prescribed limits. In no other East European state has a member of the Politburo been at the head of the Foreign Ministry as in Poland since 1956—first Rapacki and since 1969 Jedrychowski. This can be taken as a sure indication of the importance attached to its international position by the Warsaw Pact's largest state (after the Soviet Union). Poland's foreign policy can only be fully understood if it is seen as partly an expression of self-awareness and the urge for recognition. The often quoted dictum that 'in the East they call us the West and in the West the East' does not merely describe the awkward situation of a nation between the front lines. It also contains a certain pride, and the claim to be an intermediary between East and West. Poland feels itself to be a European country and would like to play a part in European politics. It is here that Poland's efforts in the field of European security have one of their roots.

The series of proposals emanating from Warsaw is well known:

(1) The Rapacki plan for a nuclear-free zone in Central Europe, officially put forward on 2 October 1957 and then amended in three later versions and eventually reduced to the Gomulka Plan of February 1964, which envisaged only a 'freeze' of nuclear weapons.

(2) Similarly in 1964 the Polish Government proposed to the UN General Assembly an all-European conference to deal with 'the whole range of problems of security and co-operation in Europe'. Two years later they repeated this invitation in the same forum. Gomulka came back to it again in his speech to the Party Congress of November 1968, some months, that is, before the Warsaw Pact states, at their meeting in Budapest, made a conference on security and co-operation part of their programme.

(3) In April 1967, at the Karlovy Vary meeting of European Communist Parties, Gomulka urged a multilateral treaty on renunciation of force and non-interference. And he came back to this idea several times on later occasions.

In principle all these proposals were neither new nor original. None the less they give revealing hints here and there. The Warsaw Pact states proposed in a declaration as early as 28 January 1956 that both parts of Germany be kept free of atomic weapons and a zone be created in which the strength and stationing of forces would be fixed. Two months later the Soviet representative at the UN disarmament negotiations combined the two projects. He proposed 'to create in Europe a zone of arms limitation and inspection, covering areas of both parts of Germany and of neighbouring states'.[47] This whole zone, not only the two parts of Germany, should be nuclear-free. When Rapacki took up the idea again a year and a half later, he declared that his country was ready to adhere to such a zone. The Czechoslovak Foreign Minister followed with a corresponding declaration on

[47] Hermann Volle/Claus-Jürgen Duisberg: *Probleme der Internationalen Abrüstung*, Frankfurt a.M./Berlin: Metzener Verlag, 1964, I/II, p. 508.

behalf of his own country. Thus the undefined Soviet formula 'areas [i.e. parts only] of neighbouring states' was extended to the entire territory of Poland and Czechoslovakia, undoubtedly an event of political significance. When Rapacki identified the Eastern boundary of the nuclear-free zone with the Eastern frontier of Poland, he made this plan an element of Polish policy to a much greater extent than in the Soviet proposal.

The idea of an agreement between all European states on security, and for economic, scientific and cultural co-operation, is also an old one. Back in July 1958 Moscow sent a draft treaty on these lines to European governments and to Washington. And proposals for multilateral agreements on renunciation of force have been part of Soviet policy since 1955. But all this does not mean that the Poles did not make their proposals on their own initiative. No doubt they were agreed in advance with the Soviet Union, but then no member of the Warsaw Pact can undertake a diplomatic offensive on this scale without fitting in with the policy of Moscow. What is remarkable in the Poles' activity is less the content of their plans than the unfailing consistency with which they pursue them whenever the situation permits. The Poles put forward and seek support for their proposals with a pertinacity and readiness for compromise that is understandable only if they are acting in their own cause. The timing at least of some initiatives shows that Moscow only tolerated them, but hardly suggested them.

The aims of the Rapacki plan, and of all European conferences or agreements, must then to a large extent be regarded as Polish aims. of what do these aims consist? A nuclear-free zone would naturally be of immediate benefit to Poland's security. Keeping the *Bundeswehr* away from nuclear weapons, and nuclear disarmament of the Americans in West Germany, would be bound, in Warsaw's view, considerably to reduce the danger of nuclear war. At the same time there is the consideration that an international system of inspection and control would set limits to Bonn's military freedom of action.

Warsaw has specified a further aim for such a zone.[48] It should improve the international atmosphere and 'make easier wider discussions on disarmament and the solution of other contentious international questions'. Conversely 'continuation and extension of nuclear armaments' would be bound 'to lead . . . to a further hardening of the division of Europe into opposed blocs'. Foreign Minister Rapacki argued before the United Nations, on 2 October 1957, for an 'effective system of collective security . . . which would take the place of the existing division of Europe'. Thus the objective is to overcome the East–West division of Europe, and the method is to approach this goal gradually through regional agreements.

[48] See the Polish Memorandum of 14 February 1958.

Warsaw's third intention in connection with this project could not be stated publicly. *Détente* loosens the bonds within the blocs, and creates more freedom of movement for individual states. Loosening up and eventual dissolution of the bloc itself would mean independence in relation to the super-power. This would bring about, or so at least many Poles think, an increase in security against intervention by Moscow. Even Russians occasionally express the idea that 21 August 1968 would have been unnecessary had there already existed an all-European security system. Dubious as this theory may be (even East Europeans are sceptical in many ways), it is illuminating all the same. The less the Soviet Union fears that internal changes in an allied country may be exploited as a weakness by the West, the less will it feel obliged to restore the balance by force.

Two further considerations enter in here. If a zone of limited and controlled armaments were created by agreement between NATO and the Warsaw Pact, a Soviet armed intervention in this zone would no longer be an internal bloc matter. It would violate the East–West agreement since it would upset the East–West balance laid down in the treaty, by introducing Soviet troops. On 21 August 1968 the Western allies could and had to content themselves with calculating whether the military balance had been damaged and whether counter-measures were needed. The intrusion of Soviet divisions into a zone of *détente* would require from the West diplomatic, political and perhaps military action. Of course it is not very likely that the danger of such complications would deter Moscow from a step it regarded as indispensable. Certainly however it would be a restraint and would supply an important argument to the doves in the Soviet Politburo.

In addition membership of a zone controlled by East and West would be bound to confer a certain special status. Even though loyalty to the former system of alliances remained the first priority of members they would nevertheless be subject to new obligations which they could, if they wished, use to build up a greater independence. The absolute division between East and West would be softened. In the long term at least, it would seem conceivable that the European states might become further differentiated. To the existing three groups— neutral, NATO, and Warsaw Pact—there would be added a fourth, its status somewhere between bloc membership and neutrality. Of course the more probable such a development seemed, the more likely it is that the super-powers, concerned about discipline within their respective alliances, would restrict rather than support the formation of such a zone, or at least its development.

An all-European conference, and agreement on renunciation of force, are linked for Warsaw to considerations pointing in two directions. On the one hand both would strengthen the *status quo* by underlining the finality of the western frontiers of Poland and the

GDR, and of the Socialist character of the Warsaw Pact states. On the other hand, according to the Polish view, meetings and agreements between Europeans on both sides would be bound to improve the East–West climate. They could form the beginning of a *détente*, with all the consequent advantages hoped for in Warsaw.

Planning for the Future

A further comparison with the GDR leads to the conclusion that for the Poles also support from the East is and remains the first require-ment of their security policy. In contrast to East Berlin, however, Warsaw would like to base its security not only on the military deterrent power and political cohesion of its own camp but also on a settlement with the West. This desire is all the more revealing if one remembers that from the Polish viewpoint threats to peace come not only from the West, but exist also in the confrontation of the two military blocs. It is however generally agreed in Warsaw that the idea of abolishing the blocs without putting anything in their place is not worth discussing. Bilateral alliance with the Soviet Union, and indeed with the GDR and Czechoslovakia also, is regarded as indispensable for the security of Poland.

It is not clear whether these bilateral guarantees could be given up within a European security system, if only because no more than vague ideas of the structure of such a system are current in Poland. Its preconditions are laid down: that the super-powers do not want war, and European frontiers are recognized. So too are its objectives: to prevent military conflicts, to preserve the existing social and political order in Eastern Europe, and to keep the balance against the growing power of the Federal Republic. But how the security system everyone talks about is to achieve these objectives no one is able to say. Whether for example one should go back to the old Soviet model—guarantees from each to each against all—and trust in that, is a question that had still not been answered in Warsaw by the early 1970s. It does indeed seem as if the Poles mean business with their plans. But scepticism, or rather realism, leads some to doubt whether any arrangement is conceivable that would satisfy both East and West. Accordingly people in Warsaw are inclined to proceed pragmatically, to work out acceptable partial solutions with both sides, and in this way set going a process of lessening the conflicts and resultant dangers.

The Poles have concerned themselves with disarmament questions more than all the other Soviet allies. The various versions of the Rapacki plan go to prove it, as do the bilateral discussions Warsaw held in the mid-1960s with small NATO countries, above all with Belgium. It is true that the objectives aimed for in Warsaw are modest. To begin with it no longer seems thinkable to the Poles to 'freeze' nuclear arms and conventional troop strengths, possibly in the

'Rapacki zone'. And it is in any case questionable whether the Soviet Union would submit to control over such limited measures. In the past Moscow has only been ready to accept inspection of agreed disarmament measures but not of a freeze on existing armaments.

The main objective of the Rapacki plan, to keep the Federal Republic away from nuclear weapons, seems to many Poles to have been reached with the signing and ultimately the ratification of the nuclear Non-Proliferation Treaty in Bonn. None the less there were signs during 1969 that a new version of the plan was being considered in Warsaw. It would have three distinctive features.

(1) Recognition that the best that can be got through NATO is a limitation of nuclear weaponry, not a total de-nuclearization of the West German area.

(2) A widening of the 'Rapacki zone', perhaps to the Benelux countries or Denmark.

(3) Special close economic co-operation within the zone.

Only time will tell whether such a plan will ever take shape and be put forward. It seems doubtful whether Moscow and East Berlin would agree with it. None the less it reveals a new direction in Polish security policy. Economic co-operation is intended, not indeed to replace military agreements but to complement them. Here too it is a question of a policy for the whole Warsaw Pact, most recently expressed in proposals for a European security conference which is to serve the interests of 'security and co-operation in Europe'. But Polish politicans display a special concern here. As one of them has remarked, 'One ought rather to say, co-operation and security.'

This shift of emphasis has two sources: a lessening of the acute security need, and the growing Polish desire for economic links with Western Europe, especially West Germany. There is an inner connection between the concepts of 'co-operation' and 'security'. Not only the Poles but all member countries of the Warsaw Pact, and to some extent even the Soviet Union, believe that the two have an effect on each other. More security makes possible more co-operation, and more co-operation creates more security. The effect of economic co-operation on security policy is seen as both short- and long-term.

Trade is able to continue to a significant extent and even expand despite political tensions, as is shown especially by West German exchanges of goods with Poland and the GDR. *Co-operation*, however, requires and promotes better political relations—or so at least it is believed in Warsaw. According to this theory economics carry over into politics after a certain point.

The long-term prospects of better economic links between Eastern and Western Europe depend on overcoming the deepest division between the two parts of the continent. Many, though not all, of the contradictions and difficulties that at present determine this relationship do not spring from ideological differences but from the different degree of industrial and social development. The poorer countries of the Warsaw Pact need protection against the West largely, though not solely, because of the historically conditioned difference in living standards. The dictatorial and bureaucratic forms of government in Eastern Europe are also to some extent bound up with this. An economically satiated country can be more liberally governed. Where the people are reasonably satisfied with their standard of living, the regime can allow more contact with other countries. As a Pole said in this connection, 'If an Englishman goes to America to work, it is no crime.' What is meant here is something one often hears in Eastern Europe. Freedom from restrictions can only be maintained between areas whose conditions of life are not too sharply different.

So far as the security policy of Poland and the other East European states is concerned, this means that the ideological danger will be reduced (not entirely but largely) to the extent that the gap in living standards compared with Western Europe is reduced. Growing economic co-operation with Western Europe helps to reduce this gap and is therefore, in the long run, a policy making for security. If the emphasis of Warsaw's policy seems to have shifted from military measures to economic agreements with the West, this has not arisen simply out of a resigned appreciation that strict limits have been imposed on any disarmament in the future. It is also a question of recognizing that danger to Poland can hardly be seen any longer in armed attack by the West, but in the phenomena of political and ideological dissolution aroused or reinforced by Western example.

In Warsaw as in East Berlin there seem to be different views on how far one should take the risk of an opening to the West. For example, the agreement with the Federal Republic is not universally approved in the Polish capital. It is true the professional arguments of economists and foreign policy specialists carry a great deal of weight, and Gierek has proclaimed his determination to continue Gomulka's Western policy. But whether collaboration with Western Europe can be regarded as Poland's long-term security concept will depend on internal developments within the country. The disturbances leading to Gomulka's fall in December 1970 have shown how many unknown factors may play a part here.

CZECHOSLOVAKIA

> One thing I will never forgive the Russians—that
> they had the Germans march in with them on 21
> August.   (An old Czech Communist, 1969)

I. THE HISTORICAL BACKGROUND

The Lessons of the 1930s

Czechoslovakia is a small state, in Central Europe, with an ethnically mixed population. These three facts together form the inescapable starting point for any security policy in Prague. A small country can seldom survive without external support, even when its geographical and political situation is favourable. A state lying in the middle of a continent, with five neighbouring countries (six after World War II) feels impelled to seek alliances. This is all the more so when the presence of national minorities excites the cupidity of neighbouring states and tension between the two main peoples, the Czechs and the Slovaks, offers an invitation to enemies to exploit this rivalry.

Between the world wars the young state sought to preserve itself by alliances on all sides. Above all it united with Yugoslavia and Rumania against Hungarian revisionism. Through alliance with France this Little *Entente* was supported by the greater *Entente* between the French and the British, which aimed at preserving unchanged the entire post-war order in Europe laid down by the Versailles and St. Germain treaties. Foreign Minister Beneš, in response to Hitler's policy of rearmament, extended the network of security treaties to the Soviet Union, in close co-operation of course with France. In May 1935 Paris and Prague concluded almost simultaneously treaties of assistance with Moscow. The Soviet–Czechoslovak treaty was limited by a revealing clause. The obligation to give assistance was only to take effect if help was also supplied by France. Thus Moscow was empowered and obliged to come to the aid of Czechoslovakia only if Paris had already done so.

This system of alliances collapsed before Hitler's threats. When the crisis came, Czechoslovakia was abandoned by its West European allies and forced to accept the degradation of becoming an object of great power agreements. At Munich Chamberlain and Daladier hoped to secure peace at the expense of Prague. Six months later they stood idly by while Hitler liquidated Czechoslovakia as a state, turning the Slovak part into a satellite and the Czech part into a 'protectorate' of the German Reich. Only the Soviet Union had offered military help — whether this was backed by real readiness to go to war cannot, of course, be known.

The lessons learnt in Prague and Bratislava from the events of 1938 and 1939 were the same as in Poland:

(1) The Germans are the main enemy.

(2) In a crisis an alliance with the West is quite useless.

(3) Firm support from the Soviet Union is indispensable for the survival of Czechoslovakia.

Post-War Policy

As early as 1943 Edvard Beneš, head of the government-in-exile formed in London, signed in Moscow a 'treaty of friendship, co-operation and mutual assistance' which was to offer protection from future German aggression and to regulate relations with the Soviet Union in the post-war period. In accordance with Stalin's wishes Beneš took the opportunity to come to an agreement with the Czechoslovak Communists living in Moscow about their entry into the post-war government.

According to the ideas of the 'bourgeois' politicians, this domestic compromise between democrats and Communists would be paralleled in foreign policy by a central or even mediating position. Beneš was anxious to avoid a one-sided link with the Soviet Union. Already during the war a plan for Czechoslovak–Polish confederation had broken down, mainly because of Moscow's opposition.[1] But in May 1946 Prague formed an alliance with Belgrade, its old partner from the days of the Little *Entente* — primarily against Hungary. More important were attempts to link up with Western Europe, despite the profound disappointment of 1938. Already in June 1946 Foreign Minister Jan Masaryk submitted to the French Government a draft treaty of alliance. A year later the Prague Cabinet decided unanimously to accept the invitation to the Marshall Plan conference in Paris. Both projects broke down in July 1947 however in face of Stalin's objections. A five-year trade treaty with Moscow took the place of American aid.

Czechoslovakia lay in the Soviet sphere of influence, according to wartime agreements between the allies. It did indeed have an alliance securing it against a revival of the German danger, but its freedom of manœuvre was restricted and becoming ever more so. Like Warsaw, Prague had to pay a price in territory. The Carpatho–Ukraine was

[1] P. Wandycz, 'Recent Traditions of the Quest for Unity, Attempted Polish–Czechoslovak and Yugoslav–Bulgarian Confederations 1940–1948', *Semaine de Bruges 1969* (unpublished MS).

transferred to the Soviet Union—it is true that only a few Czechs and Slovaks lived there. Unlike Warsaw, however, Prague had an uninhibited relationship with its massive new neighbour. (The Soviet Union has only bordered on Czechoslovakia since World War II.) Whether in the past there had really existed important Pan-slav sympathies such as were alleged and propagated after 1945, may be disputed.[2] But the fact remains that apart from Bulgaria, Czechoslovakia is the only one of Moscow's European allies whose history is not burdened with conflict with Russia and the Soviet Union. At the end of the war the Red Army liberated four-fifths of Czechoslovak territory, and gratitude and friendship towards the liberators were genuine.

The Soviet alliance was also favoured by the fact that the Communist Party of Czechoslovakia was stronger than the Communist Parties of other East European countries, even before the war (again with the exception of Bulgaria). The chief proponents of close friendship with the Soviet Union therefore had a broader base among the population than was the case elsewhere.

Prague's security policy has a threefold historical basis:

(1) Like the Poles, the Czechoslovaks solved their internal German problem after the war by the expulsion and almost complete emigration of the Sudeten Germans, who made up some 28 per cent of the population.

(2) For the Czechoslovaks non-recognition of the Munich agreement, like recognition of the Oder–Neisse frontier for the Poles, became the decisive question in relations with Germany. But an important difference should be noted. For the Poles it is a question of seeing confirmed their acquisition of formerly German territory. For Czechoslovakia it is only a matter of German acquisition of former Czechoslovak territory being declared irrevocably invalid. Germany's frontiers of 1937, upon which the Big Three based themselves at Potsdam, as did successive West German governments up to the end of 1966, included the Western districts of Poland, but not the Sudeten areas. The nullification of the Munich agreement has never had the same importance as the Oder–Neisse problem.

(3) The German occupation after 1939, oppressive and degrading though it was, exacted far fewer victims from Czechoslovakia than from Poland, Yugoslavia and the Soviet Union.

The net result for Czechoslovakia was two-fold. On the one hand, conditions were more favourable to a pro-Soviet orientation than elsewhere. On the other, relations with the Germans were not so hopelessly shattered as in Poland. Despite the bad experience of

[2] Fritz Beer, *Die Zukunft funktioniert noch nicht*, Frankfurt am Main 1969, pp. 216–17. See also the succeeding pages for relations with Russians and Germans.

Munich, the Czechs (more than the Slovaks) felt themselves more strongly linked to Western Europe, by tradition and level of industrial and cultural development, than did most other peoples in the Soviet sphere.

II. DANGERS

The Danger of War and the Ideological Threat

In Czechoslovakia there are no fears of military attack from the West —or at least there are no longer. Among some conservative politicians and older people in the Sudetenland traces of insecurity may remain. The Washington–Bonn axis is felt to pose a threat of war only in the event of 'militaristic' groups coming to power simultaneously in the United States and the Federal Republic—'a Goldwater and a Strauss, perhaps'. Statements about an 'aggressive' NATO appear comparatively rarely in the press and political speeches, even after August 1968 and April 1969 (Husák's assumption of power). Their significance seems to be quite slight—mostly it is a question of repeating old formulas, or of trying to keep in line with Soviet statements.

The military blocs are occasionally described as the 'great danger'.[3] This certainly has something more behind it. If people in Prague do believe that a military clash between NATO and the Warsaw Pact is possible, this would be because of some conflict in which the great powers were involved, probably outside Europe. Besides, it is thought that neither Washington nor Moscow wants war and that mutual deterrence is working. So there is little fear that the foci of crisis in Europe, above all Germany and Berlin, will become so inflamed that they create a danger of war.

Czechoslovakia's security problem is limited—in relation to the West—to fear of ideological diversion and economic dependence, and the weakness of a small country in face of the political predominance of its great West German neighbour. Of course, with the dismissal of the reformers, opinions about the extent of the danger of ideological insecurity have very much changed. What Dubček and his friends regarded as tolerable, their successors would consider recklessness or irresponsible lack of vigilance. All the same Husák seems to have summed up the ideological threat, particularly its extreme aspect, with notable realism. Of course he has warned that one should not 'underestimate the political influence and propaganda of the Western bourgeois countries'[4] and he has recalled that 'the capitalist world begins at our Western frontiers, a world that has not been kindly

---

[3] *Pravda* (Bratislava), 10 April 1969.
[4] To the Central Committee plenary meeting 12 March 1969.

disposed towards us in the past, and is no more so today'.[5] But Husák considers, quite correctly, that the real problem is not attacks and temptations from abroad, but susceptibility and vulnerability to these at home. Thus he reproaches the 'former party leadership' with having let it happen that 'noble ideas, which the Communist Party has always carried on its banner, have been seized upon by the enemy and misused against the Party and against Socialism'.[6] Husák's main problems are, therefore, not attacks and temptations from abroad, but proneness and receptiveness to them at home.[7]

Relations with the Germans

The Germans are traditionally the arch enemy of the Czechs. Czech history could be defined as a permanent conflict with the Germans, for a long time primarily with the Habsburgs. In 1945, however, this changed. Germany was conquered, divided, and tied to the West. Conservative Communists may well still really believe a German danger exists. But in general, since the beginning of the 1960s, people have laughed at the suggestion of a threatened German attack.

This thumbnail sketch, made by a scholar in Prague in 1969, needs some additions and slight corrections. In the first place the Germans are very much more of a problem for the Czechs than for the Slovaks, for historical as well as geographical reasons. However the historical conflict between Czechs and Germans was moderated by cultural links and cross-fertilization much more than was the case between Germans and Poles.

Since 1949 the Czechoslovaks have had to deal with two Germanys, a 'good' and a 'bad' one. This has meant that propaganda was no longer directed against 'the Germans' (which would have hit the GDR as well), but only against the *'revanchist'* Germans in the 'imperialist camp'. This concern for East Berlin indirectly and unintentionally benefited the Federal Republic. Certainly the East German Communists did enough to keep alive old ideas and prejudices. It was reassuring for the Czechoslovaks to have an allied German state on their northern frontier at least. But from the beginning of the sixties, when a certain relaxation developed in intellectual matters, and then in tourism, the Czechoslovaks encountered in East Berlin an intolerance and dogmatic narrow-mindedness that was felt to be typically German. From the discussion of Kafka, when Prague finally reached the point of reclaiming for Czech literature one of its greatest writers, to the demands for control over West German visitors and their

---

[5] In a speech on 19 August 1969.
[6] In an interview with *Rudé Právo* on 5 April 1970.
[7] See the interesting speech of 19 August 1969.

contacts with East Germans, the Czechoslovak leadership had to contend with criticism and demands from East Berlin which at times were felt to be interference in their internal affairs. Even Novotný's relations with Ulbricht deteriorated, and only the carefully conformist policy of the Czech Party leader largely concealed this development from the public. In the summer of 1968 Radio Prague produced the statement that 'it is precisely *Neues Deutschland* which chooses to remind us today of Lidice and Terezin. At the same time our colleagues in the GDR completely forget that they belong to the same nation that has Lidice and Terezin on its conscience.'[8] The participation of the *Volksarmee* in the invasion of 21 August pushed hostility to the GDR to its peak. I will never forgive the Russians for having the Germans march in with them, were the words of one old Communist. And another described how the day before the occupation he had emphasized to some West Germans that whatever might be said against Ulbricht the GDR, in contrast to the Federal Republic, posed no kind of threat to Czechoslovakia.

The next day he knew better, and so did the whole of Czechoslovakia. The 'good' Germans had turned out by no means so good, and the 'bad' no longer seemed so bad. On the contrary, they mostly showed genuine sympathy for the fate of Czechoslovakia. Of course this development must not be allowed to conceal the fact that the Federal Republic will continue to be a source of anxiety in Prague, for both the present and future regimes.

Frontier problems play an even smaller part in this. No West German government has ever made territorial claims on Czechoslovakia, or even hinted at them, and Erhard, as Federal Chancellor, was already saying that the Munich agreement had been set aside by Hitler himself. However Prague's not very meaningful demand that Bonn declare this agreement invalid 'from the beginning' complicates relations with West Germany. It gives rise in the Federal Republic to legal reservations, mostly exaggerated, which again arouse suspicion among the Czechoslovaks that the West Germans are not willing to accept, finally and unambiguously, the results of World War II.

On top of this memories of the German occupation have remained fresh, though by the end of the 1950s fears of a repetition were already gradually fading. Anxiety was kept up in Czechoslovakia by the well-known clumsiness of West German policy up to the end of 1966, by the particularly radical attitude of the Sudeten German organizations, and by all the various phenomena viewed with mistrust alike by the Russians, Poles and other East Europeans. It was feared that the Germans' national acquisitiveness, evident since the beginning of the century and expressed in extreme form under Hitler, could lead the Federal Republic into a new attempt at great power politics.

[8] Cited in *Die Zeit*, 2 August 1968.

Of course the exaggeration of this supposed danger worked in the opposite direction as well. The more contact with and knowledge of West Germans and West Germany grew during the 1960s, the more propaganda had the opposite effect to that intended—not least because this intended effect became obvious: to distract attention from difficulties at home and justify a one-sided eastward orientation by conjuring up the figure of the enemy. In March 1968 the writer Jan Procházka remarked that

> the Federal Republic is a particularly successful man-made bogey. Propaganda has created the impression among simple people that every second German is a revanchist with a knife between his teeth, who wants to plunge into Czechoslovakia at any moment. We have talked more about the Federal Republic here than about our own affairs. Anyone who wants to make a contribution to improving relations is exposed to attacks as a traitor to his country and its history. That is my opinion—and I have already once been excluded from the Central Committee for it.[9]

Since then a similar fate has overtaken Procházka once again. But the truth he expressed, which was generally accepted in 1968 when earlier propaganda was dropped, can no longer be extinguished in Czechoslovakia. 'A consumer society does not want war. And if the politicians in Bonn did want it, the Americans would stop them.' Statements like this reflect the general view and explain why, ever since 1969, official warnings against German 'revanchism' rarely amount to more than lip service to this idea.

Czechoslovakia's security problem in relation to the Federal Republic is summed up in the words of one political commentator in Prague: 'There are sixty million of them and fourteen million of us.' The Czechs often describe the Federal Republic as a great power, and for them the decisive consideration is naturally their bad experience of the nation to which this great power belongs. 21 August did not remove their anxieties about their western neighbour, but pushed them into the background. Germany is still a security problem for Czechoslovakia, but the main problem has come to be the Soviet Union.

Relations with the Soviet Union

Gratitude towards the liberator of 1945 dwindled in Czechoslovakia to the extent that Stalinism was imposed on the country. The Czechoslovaks probably suffered still more from the systematic application of Soviet principles and methods than other nations in the Soviet sphere. Their country, like East Germany, was forced down from Central European to Soviet standards. Where formerly the habits,

[9] In an interview with the *Kölner Stadtanzeiger*, 23 March 1968.

standards, and requirements of a highly developed industrial state had prevailed, now the sobriety and simplicity of a still semi-agrarian society were set up as a model. The Czechoslovaks responded with bitterness and arrogance. The political effect was described by the Party newspaper, *Rudé Právo*, in May 1968 as follows:

> Our friendship with the Soviet Union was turned into a state religion. Popular feeling turned to indifference and apathy, above all among the younger generation. It became a protest that poked fun at everything which differed from our customs and mentality, laughing ironically at its expense. This was then over-compensated by an uncritical, *petit bourgeois* admiration for all the surface phenomena of the Western consumer society.[10]

At the time this was written, it looked as if the Czechs and Slovaks would emancipate themselves. It is true there were some doubts among the population whether the reform policy could be carried through to a successful end. But the leadership, with a few exceptions, and despite all warnings, believed with a certainty bordering on naïveté that the Soviet Union would continue to tolerate their policy. They thought it would be enough to avoid the mistakes of the Hungarians in 1956, i.e. to proclaim and intend loyalty to the Warsaw Pact, and to practise caution in foreign policy.

Thus 21 August came like lightning out of a seemingly clear sky. It hit many Communists harder than Hitler's policy of force—'What happened in 1938–39 was done by our enemies. What happened on 21 August was done by our friends.' Prague and Bratislava made a discovery others had made before them. Typical was the statement of a Hungarian to a Czech: 'We understand you, but the Russians certainly do not understand you. Even when they have lived in Prague for years, even as diplomats, they still do not.' Still more enlightening was a Pole's comment: 'Our Czech comrades have made a mistake. They *loved* the Russians: we *know* them.'

The results are well known—first embittered resistance, then dull resignation; among the people conviction that only withdrawal of Soviet troops could alter the situation; in the Party doubts whether they would again be able to evoke any response from the population if they did not succeed in obtaining a Soviet withdrawal. The Czech Communists had preserved, even through the Stalinist period, an awareness of their own identity that gave them the feeling of having freely chosen to be allied to the Soviet Union. They knew of course that they could not 'build' Socialism in their country without the Soviet Union. But after the occupation many wondered whether they could manage it *with* the Soviet Union.

The comparison with 1938–39 comes up everywhere. Older people

[10] Cited in Fritz Beer, *op. cit.*, p. 190.

feel they have been taken back thirty years, and the younger ones for the first time truly understand what the old were always talking about when they spoke of occupation and repression. The comparison has a specially depressing effect when applied to the future. After 1939 the Czechoslovaks could hope for an allied victory and liberation. Now, on the contrary, many people are afraid the country may be tied to the Soviet Union not only politically but also in its rate of development. It seems that a reform policy like that of 1968 would only be thinkable again if the now backward Soviet Union itself became ready for a modern, liberal Socialism—'in ten to fifteen years' time'. In no East European capital is there more speculation over possible changes in the Kremlin than in Prague. There is too the constantly repeated opinion that Khrushchev would not have used Soviet troops in 1968. Both spring from the same desperate hope—if in the past there was a Soviet leader who would have tolerated a reforming Socialism in Czechoslovakia, then perhaps it will not be necessary to wait for decades until there come to power in Moscow intelligent people who will allow the Czechs and Slovaks to develop in their own way.

There have been and remain more immediate dangers—indirect pressure, direct activity by Soviet organizations in Czechoslovakia, renewed intervention by Soviet troops, the setting up of a military government. It may be a matter for argument how far these are still security questions. But if security means more than protection against enemy invasion, and includes the preservation of at least a relative independence, then Prague's relationship to Moscow after 21 August is an immediate security problem.

III. SECURITY POLICY

Basic Principles

The idea of neutrality for Czechoslovakia was nowhere seriously considered, outside certain small groups, before 21 August. After the occupation it became for a while quite popular as an expression of helpless indignation. But any realistic thinking in Prague and Bratislava starts with the assumption that Czechoslovakia cannot be neutral. The question of whether it wishes this does not arise. And since the events of 1968, Czechoslovakia's room for manœuvre in foreign policy has been reduced to an extent that precludes it taking any steps on its own for a long time.

Alliance with Moscow and integration into the Eastern camp form unalterable preconditions for all ideas on security. But even after 21 August, this was not just something that had to be. Despite all the limits Moscow puts upon any Socialist development attuned to Czechoslovak conditions, many convinced Communists wonder whether Czechoslovakia could remain a Socialist state in the long run without the support of the Socialist camp. Anxiety about the drawing power of the West persists even when the capitalist states maintain convincingly that they do not want to change the economic and social order in Czechoslovakia. And the leading group in power since April 1969 knows something else as well—without Soviet protection their regime would be swept away overnight.

Without guarantees from Moscow, Czechoslovakia's international destiny would also be doubtful, and that not only in the eyes of the post-Dubček regime. The memory of Munich, that 'symbol of betrayal' (Husak) lives on. Security against the Germans is still indispensable. Some people still believe this necessitates an alliance with the Soviet Union, and with Poland and the GDR. And almost everyone agrees it requires.

(1) The continuation of the partition of Germany.

(2) A guarantee that the Sudeten Germans will never be given the opportunity to return. After their experiences in the 1930s the Czechoslovaks, like the Poles, feel that a German minority in their country would be a source of international entanglements and dangers.

In its basic features Prague's security policy resembles that of Warsaw and East Berlin, but even under Novotný this policy was pursued with less emphasis than in Poland, and much less than in East Germany. While East Berlin and Warsaw were preoccupied with building up the alliance and felt bound to be cautious towards Bonn, Prague was inclined to draw the opposite conclusion—since we have an alliance, we can more easily afford to be open towards the West. The general immobility of Novotný prevented this tendency from developing into an understanding with the Federal Republic. All the same there was a desire in Prague which has continued since 21 August, to normalize relations with its Western neighbour, principally for economic reasons, but also as an additional safeguard for the territorial integrity of Czechoslovakia.

Security against the East

Since 21 August Prague's security policy towards the West has coincided in a paradoxical manner with its security policy towards the East. Everything that is done for defence against the 'imperialists', militarily, politically and ideologically, increases Czechoslovakia's reliability as a member of the Socialist camp, and helps to protect the country from interference by it. All Moscow's other allies have to *retain* the confidence of the Kremlin, but Prague has once more to *obtain* it.

That this is the first and most pressing requirement of Czechoslovakia's security policy is not disputed by any of the politicians, in principle at least. Thus Čestmír Císař, one of the most resolute of the reformers, declared in March 1969 that 'the most important question for Czechoslovak foreign policy is the regulation and further successful development of relations with the USSR and other Socialist countries. The importance of this question is such that it pushes all other foreign policy matters into the background.' Other countries must make their contribution to this, thought Císař, but he warned his fellow countrymen in these words:

> We must recognize our own responsibility and fulfil it. Anyone who denies this fact and tries to impose different views or another order of priorities is doing a disservice to our country and our people. Yes, 21 August is not easy to forget, and it is not easy to come to terms with it. But Czechoslovakia is a Socialist country. Its fate is indissolubly linked to that of the whole Socialist camp and it has no alternative but to seek and find an honourable place within this camp. All else is adventurism.[11]

Husák said on television, after becoming First Secretary of the Party on 17 April 1969,

> What must be done? In the first place, the main task is to lead our society out of this state of crisis. I would say that this is the general line ... We are also deeply convinced that by proceeding in this way it will be possible to solve, together with our allies and the Soviet Union, all the questions and problems that lie between us, once life returns to its normal peaceful channels. All, without exception. That is our firm conviction, and this is the line we shall pursue.

This programme seems as obvious as it is logical. Czechoslovakia had been occupied because it seemed to its neighbours to be internally unstable. Since that August Prague had been continually under pressure, because the indignation and resistance of the population had made it impossible for the country to settle down. Husak concluded therefore that relations with the allies could only be normalized 'if we consolidate the situation in our country. There is an indissoluble connection between the two.'[12]

In Prague opinions differ only on the question of how far it is necessary to go in order to achieve the desired 'consolidation' and 'normalization'. Of course what Dubček's successors have done and are doing is by no means determined solely by security considerations. Nevertheless it would scarcely be too much to assume that nearly every far-reaching decision in Prague and Bratislava since August 1968, and especially since Husák's assumption of power in April 1969, has been to a substantial degree one of security policy. The Czechoslovak leadership finds itself in a similar position here to the SED Politburo,

---

[11] In a speech to the Congress of the Union of Czech Fighters against Fascism on 25 March 1969.

[12] In an interview with *Rudé Právo*, 5 January 1970.

with the difference of course that East Berlin has its eyes on the West, Prague on the East. For Husak the first requirement was to restore the 'leading role of the Party'. Neglect of this had been the main reason for the occupation of Czechoslovakia. This meant:

(1) Removing all the reformers who had committed themselves in 1968, and filling all important positions with 'reliable' people.

(2) 'Purge' of the press, radio and television, whose free reporting and comment more than anything else had got on the nerves, one might even say on *the* nerve, of neighbouring governments. This is built into the system—where there is a monopoly of power, there can be no plurality of opinion. In a Communist country a single non-conforming article or speech has many times more weight and effect than in a country where a variety of views is part of the system.

(3) Reorganization of the Party (from which the reform movement came) into an instrument for carrying the will of the leadership into every area of life.

(4) Party control over the economy—as opposed to the alleged attempt of Ota Šik, Dubček's Deputy Prime Minister and architect of the economic reform programme, 'to take from the Party its influence over the whole economy'.[13]

(5) Restoration of the 'State security apparatus' which, in Husák's words, had been 'crippled in essentials'.[14] This point also has considerable foreign policy significance. For the Prague regime much depends on whether it is able to deal by itself with internal unrest, for example on the anniversary of the occupation in August 1969. Only a regime that has its own country convincingly under control is respected in the Kremlin and has any prospect of being allowed some freedom of manœuvre in domestic policy.

(6) But control alone is not enough. There can only be a lasting internal stabilization in Czechoslovakia if the leadership succeeds in convincing the majority of the party, and the population as a whole, that their policy is the necessary and therefore the only realistic one. The appeal to political sense, the attempt to make unpopular measures popular, seems at first sight to have very slight prospects of success. Resignation and apathy are too great, the greater part of the new leadership too little convincing, the possible limits of democratic development too narrow. Janos Kadar presided over a reconciliation between the people and his regime in Hungary—though only some years after his assumption of power—under the famous slogan'Who is not against us is with us.' But Husák has attacked the Chairman of the National Assembly during the Dubček era, who is said to have called for 'the discovery of a common language with all who are

[13] Husák in his concluding speech to the Central Committee plenary meeting of September 1969 (*Neues Deutschland*, 14 October 1969).
[14] Husák in a speech on 19 August 1969.

for Socialism'.[15] Husák on the contrary stressed that it must be a Marxist Socialism and without doubt he meant 'Leninist' also. But even Husák knows that he cannot just dictate. 'It is simply not admissible that the party as a whole, or its organs, should be afraid to express their opinions . . . I cannot simply come along and declare that this is a matter for the leadership, on which there can be no discussion. So long as people are not convinced, we must talk with them and win them over to our ideas.'[16] That sounds all very well, but whether the whole of the present leadership is able and willing to proceed on these principles, seems highly questionable.

Prague's immediate problem in relations with the five occupying states was to guard against the worst. To avoid the setting up of a Soviet military regime Dubček and President Svoboda, after the invasion, approved the Moscow communiqué with its provisions for 'normalization'. To neutralize the danger of Soviet intervention and moderate the pressure from Moscow, Czechoslovakia's politicians, especially since Husák took over the leadership, have been actively attempting to win the trust of their five mistrustful allies. The word 'trust' comes up all the time in the speeches of the Party leader, and has become the keyword in Prague's policy towards the rest of the bloc. Assurances are given that the Western frontier of Czechoslovakia is 'a western outpost of the whole Socialist community of states'.[17] Husák has told the Poles they have on their southern border 'true allies and friends'.[18] To the GDR he promised 'absolute solidarity'.[19] And the Soviet Union has been assured by President Svoboda that the Party and Government have 'resolutely rejected everything that disturbed our relations in the recent past'.[20] At the beginning of May 1970 there was signed in Prague a pact of friendship and assistance with Moscow which tied Czechoslovakia to the Soviet Union still closer than the Kremlin's other allies. On this occasion Brezhnev received the title of 'Hero of Czechoslovakia'.

In the ideological field the Czechoslovak Communist Party took over the theory of 'fierce class struggle on a world scale' and proclaimed its determination 'to stand unshakably on the Socialist side of the international class front' and to follow its 'active foreign policy' towards the West 'in collaboration and mutual co-ordination with the other Socialist countries'.[21] Defence Minister Džur proclaimed, 'We will so strengthen the combat readiness of the Czechoslovak army that the

[15] In September 1969 (footnote [13]).
[16] In an interview with *Rudé Právo* on 5 April 1970.
[17] Joint statement on the visit of a Czechoslovak Party and State delegation to the Soviet Union (*Neues Deutschland*, 29 October 1968).
[18] To the *Sejm* on 21 July 1969.
[19] In an interview with *Rudé Právo* on 10 December 1969.
[20] President Svoboda on 20 October 1969 in Moscow.
[21] Central Committee resolution of 17 November 1968.

western frontiers of Czechoslovakia will be reliably secured against all possible dangers'.[22] On another occasion Dzur professed to be developing 'fraternal ties' with Soviet troops in the country.[23]

The ultimate conclusion was drawn in the Central Committee's statement of 26 September 1969, according to which the occupation of the country 'was motivated by the interests of the defence of Czechoslovakia against anti-Socialist, right-inclined and counter-revolutionary forces, by the common interests and security of the Socialist camp. There was no question of any act of aggression against the nation, of occupation of Czechoslovak territory and suppression of freedom and socialist order.'

There can be differences of opinion about the extent to which all this was and is necessary. But the double meaning of Czechoslovak security policy seems indisputable. When the Party leadership justifies 21 August, follows an internal policy more restrictive than in Novotny's time, conforms to Soviet wishes for integration, promises military, political and ideological vigilance towards the West, and has its soldiers take part in joint manœuvres with the Soviet occupation troops, this has little to do with Czechoslovakia's security against the West, but a great deal with the security against the East. Prague has to become reliable again in the distrustful eyes of Moscow and its neighbours to be safe from their suspicions, persecutions and restrictions. Until this is achieved there can be no large-scale planning and no independent steps towards a general European security policy.

IV. PROSPECTS

Even at an earlier stage Prague showed a reserve in its Western policy. It supported the Rapacki proposals, presumably for reasons similar to those of the Poles, but hardly ever developed any independent initiative. Only after many years of hesitation was there an exchange of trade missions with Bonn in 1967, later than all Moscow's other allies. Contributions to a security policy that not only rests on the Warsaw Pact but is aimed at East–West *détente* appear more clearly only in 1968, and then in cautious form. Although by 1969 there was scarcely any more question of this, many of the earlier ideas fitted in so much with Czechoslovakia's interests that people are bound to return to them in Prague.

The trends in a modified Czechoslovak foreign policy that were detectable between January and August 1968 were primarily a result of internal developments. The alliance and collaboration with the Socialist camp were not disputed, every one of the reformers

[22] *Rudé Právo* and *Pravda* on 3 January 1969.
[23] In a speech on the twenty-fifth anniversary of the Czechoslovak People's Army, 7 October 1969.

emphasized this. There was however an attempt at greater 'flexibility' within the Warsaw Pact and COMECON.[24] The Czechs and Slovaks had certainly become conscious of what distinguished them from other countries in the Socialist camp—their democratic tradition (mentioned even by Husák in March 1969)[25] and a higher level of industrial and cultural development.[26] Thus they were trying not to be held back from going their own way to Socialism by too close a tie with the less developed countries in Eastern Europe, and to achieve closer contact with countries at a similar stage of development in Western Europe. Earlier on Czechoslovakia's higher economic level had been the cause of special burdens. Czechoslovakia was harnessed to Soviet strategies for military defence and for development aid to a greater extent than other countries. The reformers wanted to reduce these burdens and make the capacity released available for the needs of their own country.[27] Also, like Rumania, they wanted more say in Warsaw Pact decisions.[28] This had nothing to do with security policy or at least only in the sense that at that time security policy itself seemed less urgent in Prague in so far as it meant unity and strengthening of the Socialist camp. The world-wide role and maximum cohesion of the Eastern alliance no longer seemed so necessary, and ideological dangers from the West not so imminent, or at least not so much so as before.

As a result of this modified stand, ideas concerning a new form of European security were put forward (unofficially). These start with three points:

(1) Because of its geographical position, Czechoslovakia has a vital interest in a stable European order.

(2) NATO has drawn back from the expansionist aims of the fifties and is today only interested in preserving the *status quo*.[29]

(3) The balance of terror offers a questionable guarantee, since it

[24] Foreign Minister Hájek to the Foreign Affairs Committee of the National Assembly (*Rudé Právo*, 12 June 1968, also *Nová Mysl*, August 1968).

[25] To the Central Committee plenary meeting on 12 March 1969.

[26] Cf. *Rudé Právo* 30 March 1968.

[27] Hájek, *op. cit.*

[28] In the summer of 1968 Defence Minister Džur stated: 'We do not want to be merely passive members of the Warsaw Pact. Thus for example we support the proposals on the international composition of the common supreme command, and the institution of further bodies aimed at creating the conditions for a more objective discussion of all the important problems of our common defence . . . Czechoslovakia, in formulating its own military doctrine, has in mind to make a theoretical contribution also. Such a definition of Czechoslovakia's military and political role as a member of the Warsaw Pact can only lead to an improvement in the defence capability of our alliance in face of the numerous possible situations of conflict at the present time' (*Rudé Právo*, 16 July 1968).

[29] *Mezinárodní Politika*, April 1969.

can tempt either side to alter the relation of forces to its own advantage.[30]

The conclusions people draw in Prague in some ways resemble the statements of the Warsaw Pact, and Polish ideas, but in part they go further:

(1) In place of confrontation, security should be sought in co-operation with Western Europe. In August 1968, when it was not the fashion elsewhere, Czechoslovak politicians were pleading for a general European security conference.[31]

(2) Small countries could play an important part in *rapprochement* and collaboration.[32]

(3) The objective is the loosening and eventual dissolution of the blocs. This would be a long drawn out and difficult process, only conceivable in stages.

A typical plan envisaged the following stages:[33]

First stage

(a) Development of contacts in all fields between Socialist and Capitalist states, especially between the smaller countries.

(b) Normalization of relations between all European countries, especially the two Germanies.

(c) Mutual force reductions.

(d) European security conference.

Second stage

(a) International agreement on non-intervention in other countries' internal affairs, including the two Germanies.

(b) Creation of an international arms control authority with the task of overseeing progressive disarmament, especially in Central Europe.

(c) Development of international co-operation in all fields between all European states.

(d) Formal dissolution of the blocs.

After the experience of 21 August the creation of mutual confidence came to the fore, and the first phase came to be thought of predominantly in terms of inter-bloc policy.

(4) For planners in Prague a Europe free of blocs has certain 'Gaullist' features. On the one hand the super-powers are to guarantee the security of the whole continent and of their present allies (accordingly Prague values the preservation of the bilateral alliance with Moscow). On the other hand, however, it is necessary to avoid a situation that puts Europe at the disposal of the Americans and the Russians. The aim is therefore to combine equal protection for each individual country with a certain emancipation for the European states from the semi-European super-powers. Thus even a Europe

[30] *Ibid.*   [31] Foreign Minister Hájek, *Nová Mysl*, August 1968.
[32] *Ibid.*   [33] L. Liška, *Mezinárodní Politika*, July 1968.

without blocs draws its security from a balance of forces and requires a long-term American commitment, because otherwise a Soviet superiority would develop and West Germany would become the leading power in Western Europe.[34]

(5) A precondition for such a new European order is a readiness of the East to renounce revolution in the West, and of the West to renounce the restoration of capitalism in the East. Respect for the political *status quo* must be so great that there cannot arise even a suspicion on either side, that its ideological opponent wants to interfere in its sphere, directly or indirectly. After 21 August there was special emphasis in Prague on renunciation of attempts to intervene across the East–West border, because this seemed to offer the only chance of avoiding acts of violence within the bloc.[35] After the experiences of 1968 the Czechoslovaks have become more aware than other East Europeans that the security of Europe is also or perhaps even primarily a political question. Almost every comment on this subject in Prague since then has started out from the assumption that the Soviet Union recognizes and fears the West's superiority. Thus security agreements are conceivable only if they take into account Moscow's anxiety lest the Warsaw Pact states be ideologically softened up by, and become economically dependent upon, the West.

(6) In Prague, as in Warsaw, high priority is given to reducing the economic gap between Eastern and Western Europe. There is continuing support for a 'Marshall Plan' for Eastern Europe, but with the proviso that the West must renounce any economic and political advantage, or the Soviet Union would not tolerate such a project.

(7) Special agreements for the Rapacki zone are still regarded as desirable in Czechoslovakia.

(8) So far as Germany is concerned, Czechoslovakia's security requires the continued division of the country but also *détente* and normal relations between its two parts. German power should not be too great, and thus this potential hotbed of unrest should be stilled.[36]

How much of this programme is still perceptible since April 1969? First, the policy on Germany certainly is. Alongside its need for an understanding with East Berlin, Prague does not want to be left out and miss its chances if Moscow, Warsaw, and perhaps even East Berlin try to make a settlement with the Federal Republic. Prague also

[34] Liska, *op. cit.*; *Mezinárodní Politika*, April 1969.

[35] *Mezinárodní Politika*, April 1969.

[36] Cisař put this particularly clearly at a meeting of the Czechoslovak National Council on 31 July 1968: 'We start with the fact that there are today two German states with different social systems, incorporated into opposing political and military groupings. The key problem for European security and for our own security is to create between the two German states mutual relations such that no situations of conflict will arise, but that on the contrary these relations will gradually become normal.'

has a further interest in exploiting every opportunity for bilateral contact with West European countries. It fears a closer integration of Western Europe as this would deepen the division of the continent and make it considerably harder to resist Moscow's pressure for closer integration in Eastern Europe. Conversely, loosening up of the Western alliance offers hopes of a similar loosening in the East, or at least of keeping things as they are. The Czechoslovak Deputy Prime Minister Hamouz declared in July 1969 on returning from a COMECON meeting in Moscow, that there was no intention of creating 'some kind of "Socialist version" of the Treaty of Rome, as this would not be in harmony with the broader interests of the Socialist economy. Nor is it our objective to promote developments that would lead to two closed economic groupings in Europe.'[37] Above all Prague is interested in any kind of East–West *détente*, either between the super-powers or within Europe, because it hopes this will lead to reduced pressure from Moscow and loosening up of its ties to the Soviet Union— in the long run at any rate. At the same time there can still be seen the earlier anxiety lest increasing agreement between the super-powers leads the small states into still greater dependence on their respective patrons.

Plans for a European security system are still put aside at present. The necessary conditions in domestic and international politics are lacking. After the Budapest appeal the newspaper *Zemědělské Noviny* wrote: 'As realists we know that there is no prospect in the immediate future of dissolution of the pacts and peaceful solution of the German problem. The time is ripe more for practical measures to build up trust than for solutions to the main problems.'[38]

[37] In an interview with *Četeka*, 18 July 1969.
[38] On 15 April 1969.

HUNGARY

> Security for Hungary means creating as much
> security as possible for the Soviet Union, so that she
> will leave Hungary with as much political freedom
> of action as possible.
>
> (Statement by Hungarian journalist)

I. THE HISTORICAL BACKGROUND

Hungary, like Czechoslovakia, is a small country in Central Europe, and its history can be described in terms of varying forms of dependence—on the Turks, Austrians, Germans, and Russians. Surrounded by five neighbouring states, it seems necessary for it to seek alliances or at least firmly based arrangements. However Hungary today differs from Czechoslovakia on three points.

(1) Strategically it is less exposed than the three northern states of the Warsaw Pact. It borders on the Soviet Union to the east, and is thus looked upon by Moscow as part of its *cordon sanitaire* and therefore as an indispensable ally. On the other hand, to the west it has no frontier on NATO territory, only with neutral Austria. Hungary belongs to the southern and less important part of the Eastern alliance.

(2) Hungary has within its borders no significant national minorities. But considerable Hungarian minorities live in Yugoslavia, Slovakia, and above all Rumania (Transylvania).

(3) Hungary was among the losers in both world wars. In 1919 it had to give up substantial areas. After 1939 these losses were largely made up, with the help of Germany. But in the peace treaty after World War II Hungary was forced back into even less territory than it held in 1937.

The conclusions drawn from recent history in Budapest are not so straightforward as in Warsaw and Prague. 'One in three Hungarians lives outside Hungary's frontiers' is a slogan that still calls forth an echo in a people with an almost nationalistic awareness of their history. The regime, and all thoughtful people, argue against it. The lesson of the past, they say, is to make an end once and for all to national and territorial disputes. In view of the indissoluble mixture of the most diverse peoples in the contested areas, such disputes can never lead to a just settlement. What Hungary should demand is protection and an appropriate cultural autonomy for Hungarian minorities in other states. In Yugoslavia and, more recently, in Czechoslovakia, this requirement is felt to have been fulfilled. But the position of

Hungarians in Rumania continues to give rise to anxiety, resentment
and even hostility.

Hungary's historical experience of the Germans is also variously
assessed. On the one hand there are memories of the struggle against
the Austrians and the consequences of joining with the Germans after
1939.

> In the course of their history the Hungarian people have con-
> stantly suffered, directly and heavily, from the efforts at 'German-
> isation', from the 'drive to the East' (*Drang nach Osten*), from
> German imperialism. At the time of the second world war
> Hitler's fascism brought upon the Hungarian homeland still greater
> devastation than ever before. The rule of the Habsburgs was
> popularly described in Hungarian as 'German'. The Hungarians
> resisted German aggression at the beginning of the eighteenth
> century under Rakoczi, and in the freedom struggle of 1848–49
> under the leadership of Kossuth. Between the two world wars the
> Hungarian Communists driven into illegality, the honest Hun-
> garian patriots of the left, struggled to prevent the Horthy
> fascists from linking their policy, in a criminal, adventurist
> fashion, to the rise of Nazi imperialism, the development of
> Hitler's aggression. At first those who ruled in Budapest at that
> time agreed to Hungary becoming economically a German colony,
> later they actively supported Hitler's attacks upon Hungary's
> neighbour, the Soviet Union.[1]

These statements present the official view. They were particularly
'official' because they were written for the twentieth anniversary of the
GDR and culminate in the assertion that 'For the first time in the
course of history a real fraternity and friendship has been formed
between Hungarians and Germans'. However, historically based
resentments, such as those described in this article, occur only among
some representatives of the middle-aged and older generation.
Stronger and more widespread is the feeling of traditional fellowship
with the Germans. Economically, technically and culturally Hungary
today is still 'German-orientated', i.e. towards Austria, the Federal
Republic and the GDR. Above all it is affected by the memory that
only during the Habsburg period, and in alliance with Hitler, did
Hungary hold or acquire a territorial position it regarded as satisfactory.
There is besides another and more substantial difference from Poland
and Czechoslovakia. The Hungarians were indeed dragged by the
Germans into a war they hardly wanted. But they were not occupied
by the Germans and oppressed as a people. Nor do they have any
kind of frontier dispute with Germany.

Hungary's relationship to Russia is burdened by an event that came

[1] Joszef Palfy, *Budapester Rundschau*, 3 January 1969.

back into the general consciousness during and after the suppression of the Revolution of 1956. In 1848 Russian troops helped to suppress the uprising of the Hungarians against the Habsburgs. But this single intervention did not lead to traditional enmity with the Russians, as happened in Poland.

To sum up, then, Hungary is much less burdened with historical inhibitions than Poland and Czechoslovakia. It had not been disappointed in the West (until 1956) and during the war was allied to Germany. Culturally Budapest, like Prague and Warsaw, looks more to Western than Eastern Europe, and still today attaches great value to being counted as part of Central Europe, not the Balkans. Hungary has had no cultural ties with the Soviet Union, but neither were there deep historical tensions with its Eastern neighbour (until 1956).

II. DANGERS

Danger of War

The Hungarians do not feel threatened by anyone, as a state and nation. A typical statement is that 'We are afraid neither of a Western attack, nor of being completely absorbed into the Soviet Union.' Furthermore the Magyars believe they have reached their territorial minimum. None of their neighbours is making territorial claims on them or has any occasion to do so. Hungary's security problem, so far as it is of a military kind, consists solely in its membership of the Warsaw Pact. As a member it would be drawn into a European conflict between East and West, and if it offended seriously against the discipline of the bloc, as in 1956, it would be in danger of Soviet intervention.

The first possibility is regarded in Budapest as very slight. 'Europe has never been in such a peaceful condition as now. The problems are the South Tirol, Gibraltar, Macedonia and Germany. Of these Macedonia is taken seriously by the parties concerned, the German question is more important, but its significance has been considerably reduced.' This statement by a Hungarian diplomat points up the general view, in the leadership as among the population. No one reckons that an East–West conflict will break out in Europe, because neither the Russians nor the Americans want or could want a war. In some people's opinion Washington does not even wish to abolish Socialism in Eastern Europe any longer—it's not worth it, one cynic said. Others do still attribute aggressive intentions to the United States but feel there is little probability of a danger to Europe arising from this. Only occasionally are there signs of anxiety lest the Americans be encouraged into expansionist activities if the Soviet Union were seriously threatened by China.

Essentially politicians and press confine themselves to non-committal generalities about the United States being 'imperialistic', NATO 'aggressive' and certain circles in West Germany 'revanchist'. But there is no question of a real danger. Signs of concern became noticeable among the population, not during the Czechoslovak crisis in 1968, but only at the beginning of the American bombing of North Vietnam, and during the six-day war in the Middle East. That a war might arise in Europe seems in Hungarian eyes almost unthinkable. The only danger, which is not rated very high either, is that a conflict in which the great powers were involved in other continents might spill over into Europe.

The official, formal, verdict on West Germany contains the same elements in Budapest as in Warsaw and Prague—the *Bundeswehr* as the strongest army in Western Europe, the NPD and other right-wing currents, the initial refusal and subsequent hesitation over accepting the post-war situation in Europe as final, and lastly the economic power of the Federal Republic, which it is feared will one day turn into political and military power. But concern over these phenomena is less in Hungary, and there is a greater inclination to take seriously the will for peace of West German politicians.

Relations with the GDR are good in the official sphere, unofficially in part rather bad. East Berlin's constant efforts to instruct, to patronize and to intervene in Hungarian affairs cause much bad blood. A typical example is the closing sentence, repeated with satisfaction, of a Hungarian official's reply to a GDR complaint: He would like also to point out that the German occupation of Hungary ended 19 years ago. Thus in the Hungarian view the German problem, apart from the falling off of great power interest, consists largely in the fact that the doctrinaire thinking of the Germans on both sides prevents a *détente*. For Budapest Germany is less a focus of danger than a source of disquiet. The Germans are not a menace, at present anyway, either to Hungary or to Europe, but they are a disturbing factor.

Ideological Dangers

All that Hungary really has to worry about are ideological dangers, which in an extreme case can even have military consequences. The memory of 1956 lives on in the government and population alike. As is well known, on that occasion Budapest went very much further than Prague in 1968. It did not simply make a cautious attempt to push its own interests within the Pact, but announced that it was leaving the Pact altogether. The 'leading role of the Party' did not merely appear to outsiders to be in danger but was completely given up as a principle. Imre Nagy's Cabinet had only three Communists among its thirteen members. Soviet intervention was not met merely with passive resistance. The Hungarians fought.

All this is not forgotten, but it works upon the general consciousness in two different directions. There is deep resentment against the Soviet Union. Almost equally deep, however, is disappointment in the West, from which many people had hoped for help before and during the Revolution. The national and democratic aims of the Revolution live on. But at the same time it has sunk into people's minds that there can be no breaking out of the Soviet power sphere and that there is no alternative to the rule of the Communist Party. The Hungarians still want Western freedoms and Western living standards, but they are ready to accept gratefully the high degree of Eastern freedoms and considerable improvement in material conditions that Kadar has offered them in the course of time.

Thus the ideological danger from the West seems less in Hungary than in other Socialist countries. The Magyars can no longer be 'softened up' because this has happened already. At the same time, however, they are in less danger of overstepping the limits set by Moscow, because they know the dangers all too well.

III. SECURITY POLICY

Since Hungary does not feel threatened by NATO and is shielded against the political attraction of Western power by Soviet interest, it can do without military efforts. Budapest does just as much as is necessary to remain militarily a member of the Warsaw Pact. It maintains the smallest armed forces in the Pact, and it may be presumed that this is in accordance with Moscow's ideas — the Hungarian army is the only one in the Socialist camp that once fought against Soviet troops. No doubt there is also a connection here with the fact that even fourteen years later Moscow has no thought of withdrawing its divisions from Hungary.

For Budapest the alliance with the Soviet Union plays a role similar to that for Prague after 1968. The population sees it as expendable and a hindrance (still more so than the Czechoslovaks, who have their German problem), but it is accepted as an unalterable fact. For the regime, however, the alliance is indispensable and perhaps even useful, because it is thereby able tacitly to justify some things that it would otherwise have difficulty in carrying through in domestic politics. The stability of the country and even, within certain limits, the popularity of Kadar, are considerable, but they rest on the assumption that Hungary belongs to the Soviet-dominated part of Europe and in these circumstances Kadar represents the best that is possible. If this assumption were ever to break down, there would be no longer any guarantee of the survival of Leninist Socialism in Hungary.

Budapest's incorporation into the Eastern camp restrains revisionist desires aimed at neighbouring countries. After the occupation of Czechoslovakia, Deputy Prime Minister Lajos Fehér gave an assurance that there was no intention of taking away a single yard of Czechoslovakia's territory.[2] He was surely thinking not only of foreign opinion but also of his own countrymen. It is known that the Hungarian troops entered the part of Slovakia where many Hungarians live. A joke going round Budapest at that time should be taken at least half seriously. A soldier writes home from Slovakia, 'Our officer says, if we are brave and good, next year we can go to Transylvania.' Vague hopes that the estrangement between Bucharest and Moscow could one day lead to fulfilment of Hungarian territorial claims are not shared by politically thinking people, but they are typical of the deep resentment against Rumania. This is prevented from breaking out and producing clashes by the order maintained by Moscow within the Socialist camp.

The Soviet alliance is not a first requirement of security policy for Hungary, but it is for a Leninist-Socialist Hungary. Besides, Budapest's security policy has always been essentially an internal matter. Kadar has achieved what Husak is attempting. He has succeeded in combining the almost uncombinable, i.e. keeping the trust of the Soviet Union and gaining that of his own people. Kadar has shown remarkable consistency in drawing his conclusions from the 'events' of 1956, as they are euphemistically termed in Hungary. He continues carefully to avoid anything that could arouse suspicion in Moscow, but has gradually carried out the aims of the Revolution, in so far as the basic Soviet rules allow. His objective here has been to create the greatest possible degree of internal consolidation. And this could not be attained, after the uninhibited outbreak of free thought in the summer and autumn of 1956, either by reverting to the Stalinist methods of government of Rakosi's time, or by large-scale democratization. Kadar therefore conducted a war on two fronts, against 'dogmatists' and against 'revisionists'. First, he did what every Communist does: he 'clarified the question of power'. Only when he had brought the country convincingly under his control could he on the one hand establish confidence in Moscow, and on the other acquire the freedom of manœuvre at home that he needed for gradual reforms.

The result, given the extremely unfavourable circumstances, has been remarkably good. At present Hungary is the country with least internal tensions within the Soviet power sphere. Liberalism and stability are there combined to the highest possible degree—for a Communist country. At the same time Budapest has long since become once more a respected member of the Socialist camp.

But the experiences of 1956 are still at work. Above all they are expressed in the great caution with which the Hungarian leadership carries on proceedings of its own. The economic reforms are above all based on technical, not political grounds and political reforms are carried out either without comment or combined with a strong

[2] Quoted from *Osteuropa* 10/11, 1968, p. 774.

emphasis on Leninist Socialism. While the Czechoslovaks, in the exuberance of the Prague spring, let themselves be seduced into proposing their way as an example for other Socialist countries too, Hungary, liked the proverbial burned child, avoids anything that might give its own methods and institutions the appearance of a model. Open opposition over awkward questions like the occupation of Czechoslovakia is dealt with by exclusion from the Party and demotion. Even a man of international stature, the greatest thinker in the country, György Lukacs, although he was before his death reconciled with Kadar, is not honoured in Hungary because he is saddled with his role as a minister in the government of Imre Nagy, and is regarded in other Pact countries as a 'revisionist'. In the politics of the bloc Hungary mostly shows itself conformist, even against its own interests. All nationalistic movements, against the Soviet Union or Rumania alike, are suppressed.

Budapest wishes not to be conspicuous, in any circumstances. Its pleasure in the Czechoslovak policy of reform, the urgent warnings Hungarian politicians and newspapers addressed to Czechoslovakia in the summer of 1968, with reference to their own fate, the efforts of Kadar to prevent the intervention, to warn Dubček and to mediate between Prague and Moscow—all this was based on the fact that a Pact country was following a similar course and Hungary was no longer in the position of an outsider. So long as the Czechoslovak experiment seemed to be going well, the Hungarians were glad to have someone still further to their 'right'. When the intervention became unavoidable, they joined in. The danger of 'infection' ranked only second or third as a motive here. The decisive point was that Budapest felt it could not afford to stand aside. People who have themselves been charged with the sins of 'revisionism' and 'nationalism' cannot afford to let any doubt arise about their repentance. However, immediately after 21 August Kadar made it known that Hungary's domestic policy would be continued unchanged, as in fact happened. But since then there has been still greater caution. Now that Hungary is once again the state standing furthest to the 'right', it continues to be the object of distrust by the Soviet Union, and the victim of numerous complaints, accusations and criticisms, especially from East Berlin.

Budapest's attitude before, during, and after 21 August is typical of its security policy. Hungary is trying to do as much as possible, cautiously and without exposing itself too much. But as soon as a crisis appears, its security policy consists in renouncing foreign policy. In order to be able to do more at home, Budapest is inclined to hold back in foreign policy, and to give way to pressure from Moscow or even from East Berlin. Some interesting suggestions on European security have come from the Hungarian capital. But these are less achievements of policy than hopes for the future.

IV. PROSPECTS

Hungary and Europe

'Budapest lies at the centre of Europe, equally far from Moscow and London, from Kiev and Paris, from Stockholm and Istanbul.' This statement from a Budapest tourist prospectus of 1963 is not just advertising. It expresses a national attitude, the claim not to belong to *one* side only.

The Foreign Minister, Janos Peter, gave an exposition of Hungary's European policy in December 1966, under the title 'Hungary and Europe'.[3] Most significant is the role Peter at that time allotted to Europe in world politics: 'In today's international conditions it depends largely upon the European countries, of different social systems . . . whether we succeed in avoiding a third world war.' Europe is responsible for world peace—this idea is undoubtedly modelled on de Gaulle.[4] At the time Peter wrote his article, 'Gaullism' ranked as a modern idea in Eastern Europe. The conferences of Bucharest (July 1966) and Karlovy Vary (April 1967) clearly aimed, among other things, to encourage movements for West European independence of America.[5] The result, probably not fully bargained for by Moscow, was that Gaullist tendencies developed in Eastern Europe, most clearly in Rumania but perceptibly also in Hungary.

Janos Peter's thesis that Eastern and Western Europe should carry 'joint' responsibility for world peace has the advantage of including the Soviet Union and excluding the United States. Thus Peter does not run into the danger of trouble with Moscow. On the other hand he only mentions the Soviet Union twice in the whole article, and then not in the way customary in the rest of Eastern Europe. The Soviet Union does not figure as Hungary's most important ally, nor as the leading, protecting power of the Socialist camp, nor as the greatest guarantor of world peace. In the picture Janos Peter outlines of a desirable evolution in Europe, the Soviet Union is no more than one European state among others. And it is only mentioned because of its

[3] *Budapester Rundschau* No. 1 (February 1967), first published in December 1966, in *Nepszabadsag*, the central organ of the Hungarian Socialist Workers' Party.

[4] De Gaulle said in late November 1959, 'Only France understands . . . that war and peace are decided in Europe. Yes, it is Europe, from the Atlantic to the Urals, it is Europe as a whole, that will decide the fate of the world. If the peoples of Europe, on whichever side of the Iron Curtain they find themselves, have the will to establish agreement among themselves, then peace will be secured. But if Europe remains split into two opposed parts, then sooner or later war will destroy mankind' (Quoted in Ernst Weisenfeld, *de Gaulle sieht Europa*, Frankfurt am Main 1966, p. 51).

[5] Especially clearly in Brezhnev's speech at Karlovy Vary.

exemplary bilateral relations with France and the Scandinavian countries.

Bilateral relations like this are the main issue for Peter. He explicitly attacks the principle on which others in Eastern as well as Western Europe base the continent's security not only for the present but also for the future—the balance of power. In his view experience shows that a balance of power policy does not prevent conflicts, it provokes them. Admittedly this policy is still followed today, but this is wrong. 'Today, in a period of danger of thermo-nuclear war, the system of alliances provided for the event of war, and the corresponding balance of power policy, are not what is appropriate, but rather collaboration between countries with different social systems, aimed at finally abolishing . . . the danger of another world war.'

Collaboration is to replace deterrence. In place of the balance of power between military alliances led by Moscow and Washington arises a network of bilateral relations between all parties. The Hungarians sometimes describe this concept by the term, originating from Yugoslavia, of 'active coexistence'. Its objects are:

(1) 'Disarmament and suppression of the military blocs';
(2) 'New economic and cultural bridges between East and West';
(3) 'An all-European system of division of labour . . . which would make it possible for the two halves of Europe mutually to complement each other, despite the differences, of principle and practice, in forms of property and social system.'[6]

The security effects of this policy can best be described in a saying of Joszef Bognar, who works closely with Prime Minister Jenö Fock: 'After a certain point, the number of common interests can reach a level at which collaboration ceases to be merely policy (sometimes deliberately decided upon) and becomes a factor that every policy has to take into account.'[7] This sentence might come from a catechism of the EEC. Let us create economic facts that no politican can any longer ignore, without seriously harming his own country. Let us create common economic factors that can no longer be seriously endangered by any political difference. The six countries of the EEC have probably already succeeded in reaching a degree of economic dependence on each other that gives them a certain independence of political vicissitudes. The long-term objective of Hungarian security policy is to create the same for the whole of Europe.

Probably it would be better to say, European policy. Naturally the Hungarians want and are working for the greatest possible safeguards for peace, but since they do not see peace in Europe as being in any way seriously threatened, other motives play a larger part. In Budapest, as in other East European capitals, much that goes under the fashion-

[6] Janos Hajdu, *Budapester Rundschau*, 2 June 1967.
[7] *Budapester Rundschau*, 30 June 1967.

able title of 'security' has little to do with security but a great deal more with the interests of Hungary. Anyone who wants to replace the confrontation between alliances with co-operation among *individual* European states is trying to secure, not only protection from military conflicts but also emancipation from the great powers. Anyone who seeks to achieve a system of division of labour in Europe as a whole has in mind not so much reducing the danger of war as the economic advantages of close collaboration with the highly developed industrial countries of the West.

Joszef Bognar, who takes a special interest in economic links between Eastern and Western Europe, has made some remarkable observations about this.[8] Bognar sees as an advantage something conservatives in all East European parties regard as a danger. He does not, it is true, subscribe to the much abused 'convergence theory', according to which the different systems of East and West are coming closer together under the pressure of industrial development. He thinks, however, that the systems need each other, because they inspire and and influence each other 'throughout the world economy and international politics'. For Bognar, an ex-Minister, a member of Parliament and professor in Budapest, collaboration between the Europeans of both sides is an economic necessity. If, he believes, the West and East Europeans do not combine their forces, the Old World will not be able to keep pace with the United States, and in the long run will be pushed down to a 'subordinate status' by Asia also. He has an important sentence here: 'Such an evolution will have least effect on the Soviet Union, because it will still play one of the most important parts in international politics as a world power, owing to its own energies, if European collaboration . . . is not brought into being.'

The concept of Europe expressed here does not, it is true, exclude the Soviet Union, but it does not completely include it either. Hungary features not only as part of the Socialist camp but equally as a European country. It has obligations to its East European allies, and yet is bound up with the Western half of the continent. Budapest's foreign policy follows the same laws as its domestic policy. It cannot afford Bucharest style independence towards Moscow, nor can it afford, in relations with its own population, a sealing off from the West on the lines followed by East Berlin.

Regionalism

The way by which Budapest would like to proceed is that of regionalism. The development of good neighbourly relations is often proclaimed by the whole Warsaw Pact. But for Janos Peter this seems to have become a favourite idea. A small country, he believes, can only

[8] In a lecture in Vienna on 14 March 1967, distributed by the Hungarian news agency MTI on the same day.

act effectively in a small framework. Thus collaboration between the Danube countries bulks large in Budapest, and relations with Austria are to be built up into a 'model of peaceful coexistence'. Of course these intentions arise in the first place from Hungary's interests, especially the desire to co-operate across the East–West frontier. At the same time the Hungarians are making a general principle of it.

Europe is composed, they say,[9] of smaller regional units. Therefore what cannot yet be attained for the whole of Europe must begin within these smaller units. Like the Hungarians in the Danube area, others should seek 'regional integration', for example the Balkan States, Poland and the two Germanies, the Baltic republics of the Soviet Union and Scandinavia. The target specified by Janos Peter is that 'the development of collaboration between neighbouring countries—whether these be of the same or different social systems—leads gradually and organically to a system of peace and security in Europe'. Europe, then, is to grow together out of individual regions. What cannot be brought about by a single act of political will is to develop slowly through a large number of single measures.

Pragmatism

These ambitious desires and plans in Budapest are of course held within bounds by the facts, and the sense of reality of Hungarian politicians. They are expressed, when the times permit it, and retreat into the background when the climate deteriorates.[10] No one regards a dissolution of the alliances as possible within the next ten years—at least since the occupation of Czechoslovakia. Also, the economic involvement of Western Europe with the United States and of Eastern Europe with the Soviet Union seems to be so deep and so much determined by economic necessities, that a practicable objective is reckoned to be at best some shifts in the situation, but not basic

[9] Janos Peter, *op. cit.* Also in an address to the Political Academy of the Central Committee of the Hungarian Socialist Workers' Party, reproduced in *Budapester Rundschau*, 20 December 1968; Joszef Bognar, *Budapester Rundschau*, 13 October 1967.

[10] Thus after the occupation of Czechoslovakia, Foreign Minister Peter no longer spoke of how it depended 'largely on the European states of varying social system, whether a third world war would be successfully avoided'. Instead Peter declared, 'The question of war and peace depends today in the first place on the relationship between the Soviet Union and the United States.' At the same time he expounded at length a theme he had not mentioned at all two years before—the importance of the world-wide role of the Soviet Union since its origin for the peace of Europe, and how the 'Socialist world system' made it seem possible for the first time in history to avoid a war. Finally the Hungarian Foreign Minister swung back from his moderate East European 'Gaullism' to a strictly Party conception of the Eastern camp. 'International peace and international security' were 'determined by the successes and strength of the Socialist world system'. *Budapester Rundschau, op. cit.* (footnotes [3] and [9]).

changes. 'Socialist integration, having regard to all-European prospects', said Foreign Minister Peter in December 1968[11]—a rather sad but perhaps also slightly defiant formula which best expresses the relative weight of the necessary and the possible.

Hungary remains interested in everything that could promote *détente* and collaboration with Western Europe and loosen the ties of the blocs. Very probably it would still be ready to become part of a special zone of disarmament and co-operation like the Rapacki zone. But it is doing little to develop its own initiative, and the desired collaboration in the Danube area is also falling short of what was intended.

Pragmatism proves to be the highest law of Hungarian foreign policy. 'An agreement on co-operation of wide effect', wrote an editor of the Party paper *Nepszabasag* in 1967, could often be of much more value for 'European evolution' than well-meaning speeches or communiqués. If Hungarian diplomacy in bilateral negotiations 'emphasized so strongly the economic and cultural aspects', it would perhaps in the long run serve 'political rather than economic goals.'[12] In foreign policy Budapest proceeds as in domestic policy. In place of spectacular actions it limits itself to inconspicuous but tough detailed work.

[11] *Op. cit.* (footnote [9]).
[12] Janos Hajdu, *Budapester Rundschau*, 2 June 1967.

RUMANIA

Imagine you were lying under a tramway, and
people came along who wanted to pull up the tramway. Would you ask them what they intended to lay
on top of you in place of the tramway?
(Reply by a Rumanian diplomat to the question,
what should take the place of NATO and the
Warsaw Pact after their dissolution)

I. GEOGRAPHICAL AND HISTORICAL BACKGROUND

Rumania is part of the *cordon sanitaire* with which the Soviet Union
protects itself against the West, from the Baltic to Bulgaria. But within
this protective belt Rumania is least exposed strategically. It does not
border on the West, only on neutral Yugoslavia, and is otherwise
surrounded by Soviet, Soviet-occupied or Soviet-aligned territory.
Rumania is the least important country for Moscow. NATO cannot
break into the Eastern alliance there, either militarily or politically, and
Bucharest cannot break out to the West. Even a neutral status like
that of neighbouring Yugoslavia hardly seems thinkable in this geographical position. On the other hand this situation also has advantages
for the Rumanians. Because they are less important to their great ally,
because it is 'sure' of them, they can allow themselves more independence of action. Moscow would probably not have permitted in any
other party what it has allowed the Rumanians to do since the mid-
sixties.

Rumania's recent experiences are comparable in the first place
with those of Poland and Czechoslovakia. Bucharest was one of the
beneficiaries of World War I, which led to the emergence of a greater
Rumania, containing a number of peoples, at the expense of Hungary
and Russia. Between the wars Bucharest, like Prague and Warsaw,
sought to secure its territorial position by regional pacts (including the
Little *Entente*), allying itself with the other 'winners' against the
'losers', Hungary and Bulgaria. Since this system postulated support
from France (and thus from the greater *entente*, between France and
Britain), the Munich agreement was a severe disappointment to the
Rumanians also. It is true that they received an Anglo-French guarantee of their territory on 13 August 1939. The coalition between Berlin
and Moscow, however, sealed their fate also, though of course in a much
less gruesome form than for the Poles. Rumania lost large areas to the

Soviet Union, Hungary and Bulgaria, and became a satellite of
Germany. It refused to take part in the war against its old ally,
Yugoslavia. But it joined in the fight against the Soviet Union, in
order to make good its loss of Bessarabia. After Stalingrad the Rumanians prepared to change sides, and in the summer of 1944, when the
Red Army had already penetrated their country, they did so. Rumania
still found itself within the Soviet power sphere, but with a hasty
declaration of war against Germany it created for itself an opportunity
of regaining a large part of its pre-war territory (at the expense of
Hungary, which was still on the German side).

For Bucharest, as for others, three things had been demonstrated:

(1) There is no relying on the Western powers.

(2) The Germans are very questionable allies. Their influence in
the Balkans, like that of Austria in the past, has been mostly damaging
to Rumania.

(3) Despite the conflict over Bessarabia, there is no future for
Rumania in following a policy apart from or opposed to its powerful
neighbour, the Soviet Union.

This summing up resembles the conclusions the Poles and Czechs
were obliged to draw after World War II. For the Rumanians the
alliance with Moscow was not only inevitable, they had their own
political reasons for it as well.

This applied particularly to the Communist Party. When the Red
Army marched in, in 1944, the Party is said to have had only some
1,000 members. In any case it was the weakest in the whole of Eastern
Europe, and the most dependent on Soviet support. It was largely
drawn from non-Rumanian groups in the population, especially in
the leadership. Only from the middle of the 1950s was the Party
leadership 'Rumanianized'.[1] This created conditions and, on account
of the need for support, even a certain necessity for a 'national' policy
in Bucharest.

As is well known, this policy is supported by the feeling that the
Rumanians are a 'Romance' people surrounded by Slavs. The results
are not only sentimental and cultural but also political and economic
links to 'Latin sister countries', France, Italy and even Spain.

II. DANGERS

War, the Germans and 'Softening up'

So far as its security is concerned, Rumania finds itself in a similar
position to Hungary. A military threat only seems conceivable from a
general war in Europe, or from Soviet intervention. The first possibility is rated as little likely in Bucharest as in Budapest. The reasons

[1] A. Helmstädt, *Bulgarien/Rumänien*, Hanover 1967, pp. 92–9.

and sometimes the examples advanced to explain the relatively peaceful situation in Europe are the same.

Nor is the Federal Republic seen as a danger, either to Rumania or to Europe as a whole. Rumania has no boundary on German territory, and the idea of an attack by the *Bundeswehr* seems absurd. A possible danger for Bucharest would only be conceivable if Bonn were to support Hungarian claims on Transylvania, as Berlin once did for a while. However this possibility is never mentioned, officially or unofficially. One reason is that the frontier is a taboo subject. Another is that Soviet power in Eastern Europe is too great to permit even a more powerful Federal Republic to exercise a *dangerous* influence.

Hardly anyone in Bucharest seriously believes that Bonn is a danger to peace in Europe. Since 1965 the Federal Republic has been Rumania's second largest trading partner (after the Soviet Union). It is said that in negotiations with Moscow on a pact for bilateral assistance the Rumanians resisted a section according to which the pact was to be directed against the 'revanchist and aggressive' Federal Republic.[2] As is well known, in the second half of the 1960s Bucharest was the only member of the Warsaw Pact to take a stand against the agitation customary elsewhere against West German 'revanchism'. And Rumania was one of the first Pact countries to argue for a policy by the Eastern alliance that would encourage, not discourage, the 'realistic' forces in Bonn. The harping on principle of both Germanies gets on the nerves of the Rumanians as much as those of most East Europeans. They feel the confrontation of the Federal Republic and the GDR to be very constricting, but not dangerous. More than any of the other allies of the GDR, Bucharest ignores conditions that East Berlin makes out to be indispensable for its own and European security.

Finally Rumania is distinguished from the other Pact members by rejecting any ideological threat, or at least never speaking of it. Such a threat does in fact seem to be less here than elsewhere. Rumania is less developed, industrially and socially, than the Pact countries to the north. For the leadership this backwardness has the advantage that they are exposed to fewer demands for liberalization or democratization than other regimes. Bucharest can much better afford, as has been mentioned, what most others can hardly afford at all—to follow an independent course in foreign policy without having to fear pressure for independence in internal policy. Ceausescu has been able to base his rule and popularity predominantly on a national policy. The internal reforms that are inevitable he can to a large extent dole out as he considers necessary. All this does not apply absolutely. Above all there is no saying how long it will last. Perhaps Bucharest has still to face the difficulties with which the other East European leaders have

[2] Ulrich Kosub, *Fünf Jahre eigenständige rumänische Aussenpolitik*, Annexe to *Das Parliament*, 12 July 1969, pp. 29–30.

already had to contend for some time. But at present and for some time to come Rumania seems to be relatively immune to 'softening up', from West or East. Not the least reason for this is that the country is kept under strict, if now somewhat milder, control.

The Threat from the East

Bucharest's serious security problems lie not in the West, but to the East. Geography alone shows this. The Germans are far away—the Russians close to. It is shown by history too. Rumania was Hitler's ally, and waged war together with him against the Soviet Union. Rumania's Communist Party made no contribution of substance to the country's liberation from the Germans and was totally dependent on Soviet support in gaining and holding power. This is why Rumania had to supply the largest contributions in reparations to Moscow, apart from the Soviet Zone/GDR, and was more closely linked economically to the Soviet Union than was the case elsewhere. If one also takes into account the campaign of Russification—which up to the mid-fifties not only gave prominence to the Slav elements in Rumania and the Rumanian language, but even extended to changes in orthography— then two things can be seen:

(1) A Soviet claim to dominance so total as to be damaging to the national identity of the Rumanians, or even to call it in question altogether.

(2) A national reaction against this, which expressed itself in a de-Russification campaign, and a sharp emphasis on Rumanian elements and sovereignty.

The excesses of the 1950s have long since been overcome in Moscow. The possibilities of putting pressure on Rumania and efforts to incorporate it securely into the Soviet power sphere have taken other forms, but they still persist. Bucharest is doubtless a sore trial to Moscow. Its lack of alliance discipline in the military sphere (e.g. its unilateral reduction of military service), as in political matters; its breaking away from Pact policy on Germany by opening diplomatic relations with Bonn; its punctiliousness in avoiding or prematurely withdrawing from common arrangements running counter to the Russian line; its readiness to vote contrary to the Soviet Union in the United Nations; in general its imperturbable manner of not only protecting its own interests but of sometimes putting forward those of the bloc in a provocative form—all this is hard for Moscow to bear, because there is always the danger that this special case will become the typical case.[3] *One* eccentric can be tolerated, but several would disrupt the whole front line.

Khrushchev, like his successors, is said to have tried the old methods, attempting to draw pro-Soviet opponents of Gheorghiu-Dej and later

[3] Kosub, *op. cit.*, p. 43.

of Ceausescu into conspiracy and coup. It is however unlikely that the Kremlin made much use of the Transylvanian question since it is bound to have an interest in upholding *all* post-war frontiers (cf. p. 67). Nevertheless there is here a means of pressure open to the Kremlin, and for Bucharest an element of insecurity. This became very clear after 21 August, when the Hungarian minorities at once demanded to be included in the Hungarian state.[4] However Moscow's most important means of discipline lies in COMECON and the Warsaw Pact.

As is well known it was Khrushchev's effort to integrate economically, and thus hold together politically, an Eastern Europe striving to diverge that caused the estrangement between Moscow and Bucharest. Had an international division of labour been agreed, in the conditions of that time, Rumania would have been to a large extent restricted to an agrarian role. When Gheorghiu-Dej and Ceausescu bitterly rejected any supra-national economic arrangement, they were not defending their country against a threat of the classical type. But they were trying to defend the development of Rumania from an agricultural into an industrial state. In the last analysis this meant securing conditions for a relative national independence.

For a state that does not feel threatened by the West, the Warsaw Pact is a source not of security but of danger. The alliance forms the basis for the most varied claims to influence, for example:

(1) Heavier burdens of arms and development aid than a state itself thinks necessary.

(2) The forming of its own army on the Soviet model, equipping it with Soviet weapons, fitting in with Soviet strategy, and even placing certain units under Soviet command.

(3) In the case of political 'softening up' having to submit to collective interrogation and criticism by other members of the Pact (as happened to Dubček at Dresden, and was to happen again in the summer of 1968).

(4) Taking part in common manœuvres, or even allowing such manœuvres in one's own country (never knowing, as the Czechoslovaks discovered in July 1968, when one's allies will withdraw again).

(5) The risk of military intervention.

The text of the Treaty gives little basis for a right of intervention. On the other hand it is obvious that the military operation of 'Socialist internationalism' only threatens Pact members. Yugoslavia, in August and September 1968, although feeling itself endangered, was in principle in a better position than Rumania. All Moscow had to fear from an occupation of Rumania was a further, if powerful, drop in the temperature of East–West relations. But an attack on neutral Yugoslavia would have had to reckon with military counter-measures by NATO.

[4] *Osteuropa* 10/11 1968, p. 782.

Whether Moscow at that time actually intended, or was considering, settling the Rumania question in a single sweep after Czechoslovakia, is still uncertain. But there can be no doubt that Bucharest (and Belgrade too) feared an attack. Subjectively at least, the security of Rumania was threatened in the most extreme form, i.e. militarily. The country had not experienced a comparable danger from any other direction since World War II. Since August 1968 at the latest, relations with the Soviet Union have been Bucharest's overriding security problem.

III. SECURITY POLICY

Presuppositions

The ideas on which Rumanian security policy rests have a Gaullist look. Bucharest is similarly convinced that the two super-powers — even after a dissolution of the military blocs — will still have a dominant role in Europe, but the medium and small European states, even before the blocs are abolished, can acquire a certain independence, and influence East–West relations. The conclusion is easily drawn. If and in so far as the alliances provide security, this security persists even when the alliances are not cultivated, or when they are dissolved. In military terms all that counts in East–West relations, so one hears it said in Bucharest, is 'what the Big Two have'. For the Rumanian leadership this means that any possible advantages to them can be preserved without any efforts on their part. These include Soviet support for their own regime (to the extent that they regard this ultimate guarantee as necessary); protection against long-term revisionist aspirations by the Hungarians; a guarantee that they will not again become a counter in the rivalry of several great powers.

This assessment of its interests enables Bucharest to concentrate its security policy almost entirely on the danger of being too greatly undermined by the power of its own bloc, or even of being attacked.

Internal Politics

Bucharest's efforts to prevent this lie in the first place in the sphere of domestic politics. More than other party leaders Gheorghiu-Dej and Ceausescu have had to pay attention to the internal solidarity of the leading group. Only firm cohesion among the rulers can protect them against Soviet efforts to bring Rumania back into line by means of a 'palace revolution'. Moreover Bucharest avoids anything that might give the Kremlin a reason or pretext for thinking that the leading role of the Communist Party and the internal stability of the country are being endangered. Of course this tight grip on power serves primarily to secure the dominance of the regime. But it is more than simply an excuse when people say in Bucharest, especially since 21 August 1968, that the security of the country requires that the Party's leading role be preserved absolutely.

The second means of internal political consolidation consists in stirring up a quite considerable nationalism. The leadership of the Communist Party is recognized by the Rumanians as their own government because and in so far as it stands out strongly for the country's interests, even, and especially, against the Soviet Union. There is an unmistakable paradox here. The Party leadership keeps control over the country, as Moscow demands, by arousing and maintaining resentment against Moscow.

The third means of securing power lies in reducing existing or threatened tensions through slight loosening, or rather limitation, of arbitrary state power, by economic improvements, and by preserving rights for the national minorities. In the critical situation after 21 August, concern over the minorities was especially evident.

Foreign Policy

(a) Loyalty and Threat

Rumania's foreign policy is much more than just security policy. It aims to develop into one of the smaller medium powers, to push on with industrialization and modernization of the country, and even to play a part in world politics and not only in Europe. But almost everything done to these ends helps the security of the country and regime, and is also designed as security policy.

Bucharest remains loyal to Moscow. Both in public and private, Rumanian politicians give repeated assurances that their country will remain a member of the Warsaw Pact for so long as this exists. There is an unmistakable intention not to push matters too far. And one can still see the Rumanians shaking their heads in incomprehension over the Czechs and Slovaks, who in 1968 wanted to go too far too fast. Bucharest sometimes defies Moscow, but it knows its limits. When the situation requires it, the Rumanian political leaders sometimes 'submerge' for a while, as at the end of August 1968, when it was clear that an occupation of Rumania was not—or no longer—intended. This however is tactical caution, not renunciation of strategic goals.

In an emergency Rumania threatens military resistance. On 21 August 1968 itself Ceausescu declared to a mass meeting: 'It is said that there was a danger of counter-revolution in Czechoslovakia. Perhaps tomorrow some people will say that here too . . . counter-revolutionary tendencies have made themselves known. To all these we say: The Rumanian people will not permit anyone to violate the territory of the Fatherland.' The Rumanian leadership backed up this pronouncement with orders to mobilize the workers' militia, call up reservists, and put all the armed forces on alert.[5] No one in Bucharest at that time could have had any illusions that Rumania would be able effectively to defend itself against the overpowering might of the Soviet Union. The effect of such pronouncements could only be to create for Moscow a considerable difference between a country which it could occupy overnight, without bloodshed, and bring to its senses, like Czechoslovakia in 1968, and one where it would have to wage war, if only for a few days. If the Kremlin, so people thought in Bucharest, had decided on military action, nothing could prevent it. But so long as the Soviet leadership was wavering and taking thought, the threat of military resistance could have some effect.

The Rumanian army plays the same ambivalent role as the Czechoslovak and the Polish. On the one hand, its participation in the defensive efforts of the Warsaw Pact serves to deter NATO. But on the other hand it secures Rumania to the East, by demonstrating Bucharest's reliability as a member of the Pact. And in an emergency it deters the Soviet Union from intervention. It is principally, though not solely, for these reasons that Bucharest tries so far as possible to equip the Rumanian army from its own sources, and to make it less dependent on Soviet supplies.

(b) Theory and Practice of Bloc Policy

An important part of Rumanian security policy consists in rendering the Warsaw Pact and COMECON powerless, so far as possible, as instruments of Soviet domination. This largely explains the theoretical principles of Rumanian foreign policy. Thus Bucharest rejects the theses with which Moscow justifies its demands for increased discipline within the bloc, and stronger military efforts—that 'imperialism' is becoming ever 'more aggressive' and the Federal Republic ever 'more revanchist'. Above all Rumania interprets the key words of Socialist foreign policy in its own way.

Thus 'Socialist internationalism' does not mean an absolute duty to subordinate one's own interests to those of the camp. It is rather a question of an obligation, freely entered into, to cultivate closer and better relations with the Socialist countries than with other states. As it was put in Bucharest—the law forbids theft but it does not command courtesy, which can only be freely offered.

Sovereignty is expounded in the same style. It is like pregnancy, either it exists or it does not. In Bucharest's view sovereignty is not determined from a class standpoint, but is as absolute as the principles of *non-intervention in the internal affairs of other states* and *respect for the territorial inviolability of other countries*. In the Rumanian view these principles must be as much respected within the Socialist camp as in the rest of the world.

[5] *Osteuropa* 10/11 1968, pp. 781–2.

Coexistence, in Rumanian usage (as in Belgrade and Budapest), is usually linked to the word 'active'. It does not mean merely tolerating states with other forms of society, but calls for the creation of the best possible relations with them. People are therefore inclined in Bucharest to speak more of co-operation than of coexistence.

In using the phrase 'security system' the Rumanians avoid adding 'collective'. Security in Europe is not to be created by an organization with the right of majority decision, but by a network of bilateral connections, as is also preferred by the Hungarians.

All these principles are undisputed in Eastern Europe, if not in their Rumanian version. For Bucharest they form the theoretical tool with which to resist the pretensions to power of Moscow and the majority of the Pact. So the Rumanian leadership defend themselves against:

(1) Any international control over the Rumanian economy, and

(2) The claim by the Pact to take part in decisions on the domestic and foreign policies of its members, to hold manœuvres in a country without its agreement, and to intervene militarily.

Consistent pursuit of this policy caused Rumania to be excluded from consultations about and action against Czechoslovakia in 1968. Although Dubček's course of reform did not much please the Rumanian leadership, they gave demonstrative support to Prague, and concluded a bilateral pact of assistance with Czechoslovakia, the only member of the alliance to do so. Just as Kadar expected to find the Czechoslovak reformers congenial friends to his domestic policies, so Ceausescu hoped that in the long run he would acquire in Czechoslovakia an ally in foreign policy, still within the bloc but ready to stand up for its own interests against the bloc's demands. It is probable too that memories of the pre-war Little *Entente* played a part.

(c) Policy Outside the Pact

Rumanian policy within world Communism springs from the same considerations. Bucharest, like all other members of the Pact striving for more independence of Moscow, is keenly interested in avoiding a formal split in the Socialist world system. It opposes any attempt by the Soviet leadership to 'excommunicate' China at a 'Council' of Communist parties, or even simply to criticize China. For once this process is started up again and, as with the Cominform decision against Yugoslavia in 1948, a majority of Communist parties is formed against another party, Rumania would have to fit in with Soviet wishes so as not to be threatened with condemnation.

But there is a further reason why Bucharest strongly emphasizes the unity of *all* Socialist countries, and maintains better relations than any other member of the Warsaw Pact with the 'heretics'—China, Albania and Yugoslavia. Skilful exploitation of the Sino-Soviet dispute is known to have enabled Bucharest to escape Khrushchev's plans for economic integration at the beginning of the 1960s. The presumptuous attempt to mediate between Moscow and Peking led, it is true, to nothing but it strengthened Rumania's position within world Communism. Bucharest's approach to Yugoslavia is favoured by traditional links from the time of the Little *Entente*, but it is based upon similarity of ideas in foreign policy. In the hour of danger after 21 August, Tito and Ceausescu quickly came together for joint consultation.

Of course, in a crisis, neither Peking nor Belgrade can protect the Rumanians from Soviet intervention. But a certain limited security effect arises from the fact that a country becomes more difficult for Moscow to attack, the stronger its position is in the Communist world as a whole.

All Bucharest's efforts to develop a role in the non-Communist world are aimed at achieving the same effect. Important examples are Rumanian activity in the UN Economic Commission for Europe and above all in the United Nations Organization itself. In 1967 Foreign Minister Manescu was elected President of the UN General Assembly. The preceding year there arose at his invitation within the organization the Club of Nine, a group of smaller European states who consult together about possibilities of *détente* in Europe. This club comprises members of NATO, of the Warsaw Pact, and neutrals. And in order to avoid a confrontation between the alliances, which means pressure for increased discipline within the alliances, Rumanian diplomacy would like to allot the neutral countries as important a part as possible in a general European security conference.

Equally important are Bucharest's efforts to establish close relations with the West, above all France and the United States. President Nixon's visit to Bucharest in 1969 was a minor sensation. Little reason though there is to deduce from it a security guarantee for Rumania, the leading power of NATO did make it emphatically clear that it is not willing to leave even Warsaw Pact countries to be disposed of exclusively by Moscow. No doubt a Soviet attack on Rumania after 21 August would not have set off any military reaction by Washington, but it seems possible that at that time Bucharest received a certain American support, in a tacit and indefinable manner.

Rumania's policy in the Balkans is a reflection of Rumanian foreign policy as a whole. Bucharest maintains good relations with countries of the most varied tendencies—with Greece and Turkey which are NATO states, with Albania, linked to China, with neutral Yugoslavia, and with Bulgaria with its strong leaning towards Moscow. The Rumanians' desire to moderate conflicts within their own region comes from long experience, still remembered in other Balkan countries too, of how quarrels between small states in the end only help the great powers. In the present-day context, this means that the South-East Europeans should not let themselves be played off against each other, either by their own great patrons or through a confrontation of the blocs to which they mostly belong. Despite all their differences they should work for a high degree of co-operation. The Balkans as a model of *détente* in Europe, as a nuclear-free zone (such as Bucharest proposed at the end of the 1950s, in parallel with Rapacki and in agreement with Moscow), the Balkans as a zone of peace—all this is still Rumania's aim, though of course only in the long term.

Results

Rumania's security problem is very like Hungary's, and the conclusions drawn by Bucharest and Budapest are similar. The Rumanians are also pragmatists. They concentrate in the first place on progress in their own area, the Balkans. In the name of European security they press for a good deal that really suits only, or mostly, their own interests. They seek protection for their country and regime not in the strengthening and solidarity of the Warsaw Pact or even in confrontation with the West, but in *détente* and bilateral collaboration with all European states. They are in favour of every kind of arms limitation, disarmament, troop reduction or withdrawal, and the abolition of military bases. They do, it is true, profess struggle against imperialism, and the unity of the camp, but they are working to moderate the opposition between East and West, and to loosen up their own bloc as far as possible. They attach importance to the Americans continuing to form a counterweight to the Soviet Union in Europe, and are clear that the two superpowers will continue to have a decisive influence on the old world in the future. In the Rumanian view regional agreements on arms limitations or collaboration should be guaranteed by Moscow and Washington. At the same time Bucharest fears an agreement between the two great powers, leaving the Europeans on either side helpless in the grip of their respective super-powers.

What distinguishes Bucharest from Budapest is the emphasis with which it pursues these goals. A Rumanian diplomat, asked what was the greatest obstacle to *détente* in Europe, replied: lack of activity. No one can reproach the Rumanians with such a lack of activity. And although they agree very largely with their Hungarian neighbours in many basic ideas, there are considerable differences in practical politics. Ceausescu does the direct opposite of Kadar. Kadar holds back in foreign policy, so as to win room for manœuvre in domestic affairs. Ceausescu, however, holds back in domestic policy, and makes reforms only very cautiously, in order to create and preserve autonomy in foreign policy.

IV. CONCEPTS OF THE FUTURE

Rumania is potentially a second Yugoslavia. This does not mean that Bucharest is aiming consciously at non-alignment, or regards this as possible within a foreseeable period. But the preconditions for neutral status seem to be further developed in Rumania than in any of the other Warsaw Pact countries. In addition the vigour with which Bucharest urges and works for abolition of the blocs is unparalleled within the Eastern Alliance. Rumania wants the dissolution of the military alliances without their having to be replaced by a general European security system. Rumanian politicians do speak of such a system, but there is as little information about its form to be had in Bucharest as in all the other East European capitals. One reason is that no one in Rumania counts on an abolition of the blocs in the near future. Another is that the ideas to be met with in Bucharest of a future Europe without blocs are different from those of the countries to the north.

Anyone who asks in Rumania for an alternative to the present situation of security maintained by deterrence, is told: 'Relations between individual states must be improved, between each and every state. Only in this way will it be possible, in time, to remove the causes and conditions of conflict, and above all the mutual distrust.' The Rumanians are aiming at the same thing as Hungary's Foreign Minister Janos Peter. They want to undercut the confrontation of the blocs by creating below the level of the Pact organization a network of bilateral connections. Whether Bucharest really wants to maintain the bilateral treaties of friendship and assistance within the Eastern camp seems very questionable. But it sees their continued existence as unavoidable. There is only one possibility of loosening these one-sided ties: to complement them by links in the other direction, with neutral and Western countries. The objective would be a Europe whose individual states were bound to each other by so many interests and obligations that military conflicts would become impossible. The blocs would not be dissolved by any decision or treaty but would dissolve themselves in the course of a long process. As the conflict between East and West gradually lost its importance, the military alliances would lose their meaning. The claim of the super-powers to domination would not be abolished thereby, but it would be considerably reduced, and the danger of interventions within the pacts would be diminished.

These objectives (which in Bucharest are not depicted quite so clearly) may seem Utopian, but Rumanian foreign policy has done more to bring them about than all the other members of the Pact. Bucharest, in freeing itself from ideological orientation in the bases of its foreign policy, has taken an important step in principle. It has passed from partisan to objective thinking. It has given up using as its ultimate standards the actual or supposed advantage of world Socialism. Only this liberalization from dogma in foreign relations can form the basis for a comprehension, understanding, *rapprochement* and co-operation between East and West.

BULGARIA

The best thing would be if the Americans and the
Soviet Union withdrew their fleets from the Mediterranean.   (Bulgarian journalist, 1969)

I. GEOGRAPHICAL AND HISTORICAL
BACKGROUND

Through a large part of its history Bulgaria was the victim of its
strategic importance. For the Turks it was the gateway to the Balkans
and Europe. For nearly five hundred years it was a Turkish province,
more powerfully subjected to Ottoman domination than other South-
East European countries. For Russia it has served since the end of the
nineteenth century as a base for its policy in the Balkans, and against
Turkey.

Even today geography to a considerable extent determines the
country's fate. Bulgaria borders on two NATO countries—Greece
and Turkey. It nowhere touches on the Mediterranean, but in places
it is only a few hours by tank from the Aegean coast, and above all it
is close to the Dardanelles. In any conflict over the straits it would be
the springboard for Soviet action. A war between East and West
would immediately involve Bulgaria. Since Yugoslavia has withdrawn
from Soviet domination and Rumania has begun to emphasize its
autonomy, Bulgaria's importance to Moscow has grown. It represents
the only reliable base for Soviet political and military action in the
Balkans. Assertions that Soviet troops had appeared in Bulgaria after
21 August were more rumours than real reports—but the fact that
such statements could be thrown about (even in diplomatic circles)
shows that Bulgaria is regarded in Bucharest as a threatening wedge,
and in Belgrade as an outpost of Soviet power.

The strategic role of Bulgaria is matched by historical connections
between Sofia and St Petersburg, or Moscow. The Bulgarian élite who
worked for liberation from the Turks in the nineteenth century were
educated at Russian universities. In 1877–78 Russian troops brought
about this liberation. At that time only Russia offered the Bulgars (in
the Treaty of San Stefano) an extension of territory into Macedonia and
Thrace to the Aegean, which fulfilled their historic claims, but was
reversed by the other European powers a year later, at the Congress of
Berlin. Russia helped to create the Bulgarian state. And Russian
officers (from first lieutenant upwards) trained and led the Bulgarian

army for a considerable time towards the end of the century. Only the hope of at last gaining the territory so often vainly striven for brought Sofia into World War I on the side of Austria and Germany, and thus against Russia. In World War II Bulgaria again allied itself with the Germans for the same reason, but refused to declare war on the Soviet Union.

The Bulgarian Socialists and Communists were Russian-orientated, by contrast with the Communists of the other Balkan countries, who modelled themselves primarily on the Germans and French.[1] Likewise, in distinction from the Communist Parties of neighbouring states, the Bulgarian Communists had already grown to be the second strongest party in the country in 1919, and influenced national policy, although for a long time forbidden. Above all, during the inter-war period they played a considerably greater role in the Comintern than the Communist Parties of other South-East European countries. Their close links and connections with the Soviet Party created for them a special position that continued to have an effect in the period after 1945.

The partisan movement—not, it is true, a very important one—and the 'Fatherland front', which in 1944 overthrew the pro-German government in Sofia almost simultaneously with the entry of Soviet troops, were Communist-inspired or led. On the other hand the Soviet Union had declared war on Bulgaria only a few days before, in order to be able to enter the country and bring it under control. The Bulgarian Communists would probably not have come to power without Moscow, or not so soon. But they had done more on their own accord to prepare for the take-over of power than the Communists of some other countries in Eastern Europe. Therefore their standing both with their own people and with Moscow was stronger.

Naturally Russo-Bulgarian relations up to 1944 had not been free of conflicts. The Tsars' help was not disinterested, and the Bulgars had to protect themselves against being reduced to a vassal state. But the close relationship of language, shared historical experience, and the lack of a common frontier (something particularly conducive to friendship), created favourable conditions for an alliance such as the Soviet Union has not met with in any other present member country of the Warsaw Pact. As a Bulgarian has said, 'We stand closer to the Russians than do some peoples of the Soviet Union.'

On the other hand the Bulgarians also have sympathies with the Germans. They lost two wars on their side, but equally they remember the brotherhood in arms, the close economic relations in the 1930s, and the territorial gains to north, west and south, that alliance with Berlin brought them. It was the Germans who gave the Bulgarians the territory they had been seeking, for the first time since 1878.

[1] Paul Lendvai, *Der Rote Balkan*, Frankfurt am Main 1968, p. 231. See this book also for the most important literature on the subject.

Bulgaria declared war on the United States and Britain in 1941, under pressure from Hitler. This was, so it is held in Sofia today, a pure matter of form. Thus the fact that towards the end of the war the Allies bombed Bulgaria is held against them, though only occasionally.

II. DANGERS

Bulgaria has no special security problem. Its history since 1879 is a story of unrealized, or only briefly realized, claims upon its neighbours, not of threats from these neighbours. 'We have always won the battles and lost the wars,' they say in Sofia. In World War II Bulgaria, like Hungary, was among the 'losers', apart from Southern Dobruja which Hitler gave the Bulgarians in 1940 and the Soviet Union left them in 1944. But there is no serious threat from Rumania resulting from this. And otherwise no one wants territory from Bulgaria.[2]

Dangers from the West

Relations with the NATO countries, Turkey and Greece, were for a long time strained. But they have become normal since the middle of the 1960s. No one in Sofia, it is generally agreed, fears anything from Istanbul and Athens. The only thing that gives rise to security considerations is the fact that these two southern neighbours belong to the Western alliance.

For Bulgaria there is a military danger only if an East–West conflict develops, or if Moscow intervenes. With regard to the first possibility, Sofia feels more exposed than Rumania, and not only because of the proximity of NATO states, i.e. Greece and Turkey. Bulgaria, though without access to the Aegean, is still a semi-Mediterranean state. When Moscow and Washington commit themselves in the Middle East, and their fleets rival each other in the Mediterranean, this concerns foreign-policy makers in Sofia more than their colleagues in other Warsaw Pact capitals. Protests against demonstrative voyages by American units into the Black Sea are therefore probably more than propaganda. Sofia's connection with Moscow forbids repeating openly the Yugoslavs' demand—that both great powers withdraw from the Mediterranean. But there can be no doubt that Bulgaria would feel more secure if the Mediterranean and the Balkans ceased to be an area of confrontation between the two super-powers.

Germany lies far from Sofia. From one point of view this means that its affairs are a matter of indifference. Bulgaria is interested in stronger economic links with the Federal Republic and the GDR. Among Bulgaria's trading partners West Germany stands first in the West,

[2] The demands of Macedonians in Skopje extend only—at present anyway —to a minority status for the Pirin Macedonians belonging to Bulgaria. For details see Lendvai, *op. cit.*, p. 266. Cf. p. 241.

East Germany second in the East. In Sofia they do not shrink from exploiting the conflict between the two Germanies, so far as bloc loyalty allows. In addition the Bulgarians feel that the quarrel between Bonn and East Berlin is an obstacle to their desire for more links with Western Europe. On the other hand, however, one effect of the remoteness of these Central European disputes seems to be that the Bulgarian leadership gives more credence to the assertions by Moscow and East Berlin about the danger of the 'Bonn revanchists' than is the case in Bucharest and Budapest. When Bulgarian Communists speak of the threat to peace emanating from the Federal Republic, it seems to be with rather more conviction behind it.

Dangers from the East

For Bulgaria the danger of Soviet intervention seems to be slight, for two reasons. First, all politically conscious people are aware of this danger, because they know the strategic and political importance their country has for Moscow. The following is a typical, if exaggerated, statement: 'If a development had set in here like that in Czechoslovakia between January and August 1968 — the Russians would already have marched in in February.' Secondly a conflict between the Soviet Union and Bulgaria is not very probable for the foreseeable future, because their conflicts of interest are less than in the relations of other Pact members to the Kremlin. Bulgaria is a kind of favourite child of the Soviet Union. After 1945 it was less plundered than Rumania, and received from Moscow more credits and economic help, in relative terms, than others did. Sofia is deeply in debt to Russia. And when Todor Zhivkov goes on one of his frequent visits to Moscow, people say in Sofia that he is going begging again. Bulgaria is economically almost completely dependent on the Soviet Union, but it is a very profitable dependence.

Certainly Sofia's ostentatious loyalty offends the national pride of many Bulgarians. The military coup of 1965, suppressed even before it broke out, was probably aimed at a greater autonomy for the country in relation to the Soviet Union. And cool though relations with Rumania are, the example of its foreign policy has an effect on Bulgaria, where the feeling of national identity has been reawakened since the mid-1960s, and has been promoted by the regime. This is not yet a serious problem in relation to Moscow, but it could become so, all the more since Stalinism and the particularly strong revolutionary zeal of the Bulgarian Communists have considerably reduced the Bulgarians' former sympathies with their Russian 'elder brother'.

Bulgarian national emotions are still particularly inflamed by the Macedonian question but there are no foreseeable prospects of realizing the main objective of all Bulgarian history since 1879. The Macedonians are aware of the advantages of belonging to liberal

Yugoslavia, and not Bulgaria, which is poorer and more strictly ruled. Besides they remember that the Bulgarians, who occupied their country in 1941, appeared less as liberators than as conquerors. Above all there are hardly any chances of it in the actual foreign-policy situation. Bulgarian revisionism has, it is true, broken out openly when relations between Moscow and Belgrade have deteriorated. But frontier changes, even at the expense of neutral Yugoslavia, would seriously disturb the reconciliation of forces in the Balkans. And this would hardly be in the interest of the two super-powers who are anxious to maintain the *status quo*. Moscow will scarcely be prepared to recreate for Sofia what St Petersburg gave in 1878.

It may be that some Bulgarians, and perhaps even Bulgarian politicians, do nevertheless still entertain some hopes here. But as soon as these hopes prove to be illusionary, the 'nationalist' reason for close friendship and almost unreserved compliance with the Soviet Union falls away. By then at the latest, the national self-consciousness of the Bulgarians is bound to be turned against what most restricts them— the Soviet Union.

Ideological Danger

The Macedonian question, like comparable disputes elsewhere, is largely a matter of generations. There is the prospect that, not soon but in the course of time, it will lose its importance. Already it can be seen that resentment against Yugoslavia and suppression of information about Yugoslavia do not prevent Bulgaria's neighbour from exercising an attraction on the Bulgarians. Bulgarian visitors go shopping in Belgrade, as Poles do in East Berlin and East Germans used to do in West Berlin, before the wall stopped them. And when Yugoslav tourists come to Bulgaria with their *flietscher*,[3] the mini-Fiat built in their country, they provide a seductive example of the possibilities open to a Socialist state. Sofia also allows into the country great numbers of Western tourists (like Hungary, Rumania and Czechoslovakia), whose influence stirs the Bulgarians to make envious comparisons with the prices and quality of their own goods. To the regime the risks seem less than the financial gain in foreign currency. On the other hand Yugoslavia sets the Bulgarians an example which seems conceivable and attainable for themselves—not only in living standards, but also in the liberalism of its internal policies. Tito's country therefore is a more powerful source of ideological danger to Sofia than the West.

The Czechoslovak reform policies of 1968 aroused certain expectations in Bulgaria also, despite the great distance. For here was a country *inside* the bloc trying to carry out what Zhivkov, steering between dogmatists and progressives, did not or could not venture.

---

[3] It has not been possible to discover the spelling of this slang word.

II. SECURITY POLICY

Bulgaria's security policy—like its foreign policy—is determined by
seeing clearly that it is a small country. In the words of a journalist
in Sofia, 'Even for the Yugoslavs and Rumanians it is hardly conceivable
that they should really play an international role. For Bulgaria it is
unthinkable.' All the regime's efforts to protect the country from harm
and keep itself in power are therefore limited to two objectives—maintaining good relations with the Soviet Union and avoiding or reducing
tensions in the Balkans.

Relations with the Soviet Union

In Sofia more is done to cultivate relations with Moscow than in other
East European capitals—probably more even than in East Berlin.
The speeches of Bulgarian politicians, the text of their treaty of friendship with the Soviet Union (and also with other Pact members), harp
on phrases like 'fraternal', 'unshakeable', 'indestructible', 'holy' and
'eternal'. The Soviet ambassador in Sofia holds an honorary seat in
the Party Præsidium and accompanies the Prime Minister when he
travels about the country.[4] Bulgaria shows itself the most faithful of
the faithful as, when and where required. It follows at once every
variation in Moscow's course, hails every change in the Kremlin
(especially conspicuously after Khrushchev's fall), supports Soviet
efforts to establish more firmly the Warsaw Pact and COMECON,
directs polemics against Mao Tse-tung and in November 1966 even
argued for a world Communist conference, whose object could only be
the 'condemnation' of China.[5] Finally, what other Warsaw Pact leader
could bring himself to say, as Zhivkov did at the 1966 Party Congress:
'We are of the opinion that our army is part of the Soviet armed forces.'[6]

This exaggeration does not, of course, derive only from considerations of security. Trotsky was already struck by the imitative zeal of
the Bulgarian Communists, and their tractability and readiness to
conform were already evident in the Comintern.[7] To this tradition is
joined the calculated intention of preserving and extending the advantages Sofia enjoys through its special relationship with Moscow.
But behind this loyalty lies the experience of most Balkan peoples that
as soon as they stand alone, they become the plaything of rival powers.
Bulgaria needs firm support—that is not only the opinion of Communists. And in the nature of things this support can only be given by
the Soviet Union. In addition, there is the consideration already

[4] Lendvai, *op. cit.*, pp. 225–6.
[5] A. Helmstädt, *Bulgarien/Rumänien*, Hanover 1967, p. 41.
[6] Quoted in Lendvai, *op. cit.*, p. 263.
[7] Lendvai, *op. cit.*, pp. 231 and 234.

mentioned that Bulgaria is too important to the Kremlin for it to be able to afford a neutral status or even experiments that might give rise to doubts of its reliability in Moscow.

At the same time the safeguarding of the regime plays a large part. Whether a more national or more liberal Socialist leadership could survive without Soviet protection is doubtful. Zhivkov could not do it, because he does not have the personality, and does not wield the same power within the Party as his predecessors, Dimitrov and Tscherven-kov. Zhivkov owes his position at the top above all to Khrushchev and to the favour he won with his successors. To hold on to his position he needs the support of the Soviet Union.

But he cannot and does not wish to support himself on this alone. A part at least of both his home and foreign policies is aimed at creating a base for himself within the country. The economic reform, which goes further than most outsiders assume, is naturally based in the first place on economic grounds. But it also secures for the head of the Party and government the support of the modern-minded, technocratic circles in the Party. Besides, it promises, in time, an improvement in material living standards.

Among hopeful Bulgarians Zhivkov is accounted a liberal, and certain relaxations since the mid-1960s should not be overlooked. But even leaving out of account the still powerful conservative wing of the Party, the Bulgarian Party leader here runs into the classical dilemma of almost all leaders in the Eastern bloc. He has to liberalize, in order to produce stability for Moscow. At the same time he has to hold back the liberalization lest any doubt about this stability should arise in Moscow. This conflict of intentions and compulsions largely explains the contradictory picture Bulgaria presents: relative magnanimity towards Western behaviour by young people, but purges in the press, radio, cinema and television, after 21 August; economic reforms that go further than in the Soviet Union, but increased trade and 'integra-tion' with the Soviet Union; openings to the West, but strengthened links to the East; awakening of national self-awareness, but intensified proclamation of loyalty to Moscow. In part, too, the Bulgarians are trying to do the same deal with Moscow as the Poles and Hungarians, and as attempted by Prague—to buy freedom of manœuvre by con-formism in foreign policy.

The same dichotomy appears in Sofia in the maintenance of foreign relations. Since the mid-1960s the Bulgarian leadership has been trying to pacify awakening national feeling by demonstratively expanding its international contacts by political tourism in Western Europe (Zhivkov was the first Bulgarian head of government to visit Paris), journeys through the third world, and activity in the Balkans. All this remains within the framework of current Soviet policy, in relation to Moscow and in fact. But it is also intended to give the impression at home that

Sofia is taking certain steps along the 'Rumanian' way. In addition, although it cannot be proved, it may be supposed that the regime regards the Macedonian question as useful for guiding national feeling, and countering 'softening up' by the Yugoslav example.

At present it would be wrong or premature to speak of a balancing act in Bulgarian policy. The Party leadership feels too dependent on Moscow to venture anything in home or foreign policy that might attract disapproval from the Kremlin. It can however be maintained that the present and any future regime will be less and less able to base its position too firmly upon Soviet support.

Balkan Policy

Sofia's Balkan policy forms the main area of its efforts in foreign policy. Like that of Rumania, it starts out from the lesson of experience, that the states of South-East Europe can only reduce their dependence on, and exposure to influence by, the great powers, and can best avoid conflicts, if they establish a certain harmony among themselves. For internal political reasons this principle is not always followed in relations with Belgrade. On the other hand there is a tradition of reconciliation with Yugoslavia in the plans of Dimitrov and Tito for a federation of the two states. The enterprise broke down, as is well known, with Stalin's intervention, and for the foreseeable future it seems to have no prospects whatever. If Moscow does not want federations within the bloc, still less will it tolerate legal ties to a neutral country. It also seems very questionable whether Sofia, at a time of growing nationalism in South-East Europe, would be prepared for an agreement that the former General Secretary of the Comintern had in mind in an excess of internationalism after the war, even if this were possible. However, since Tito's visit to Bulgaria in 1965, Sofia and Belgrade have normalized their relations.

Relations with Rumania are not very good: 'Both sides could give up trade without loss, and we have more cultural exchanges with Scotland than with Rumania.' Such statements are exaggerated, but they indicate the mood. None the less Zhivkov and Ceausescu have come to terms, and the communiques after their meetings are sometimes so packed with 'Rumanian' expressions[8] that the Bulgarian signature comes as a minor sensation. Above all, however, Sofia and Bucharest have the same goal. Both support a 'zone of peace and co-operation' in the Balkans, and their differences of opinion in this matter seem to relate mainly to the question of who has done it earlier and is doing more today.

There can be no doubt of the Bulgarians' determination to nurture

[8] For example in the Communiqué following Ceausescu's visit to Sofia in September 1965.

the forces of *détente* in their own neighbourhood. They claim to have obliged Khrushchev to approve their policy of settlement, contrary to his wishes, on a visit to Sofia at the beginning of the 1960s. They have even spoken in favour of normalizing relations with Albania.[9] More important however—and here Soviet and Bulgarian views largely coincide—are Sofia's efforts to normalize relations with its NATO neighbours, Greece and Turkey. Both native and foreign observers in the Bulgarian capital are agreed that here Sofia has gone to the limits of what is practicable, and that this has been a success. Disputes were settled, although Turkey in particular showed reserve. And Sofia maintains correct relations even with the Colonels' regime in Athens. It is said to have been active diplomatically during the Cyprus crisis, concerned lest the Greeks and Turks come into conflict close to Bulgarian soil—doubtless the only case of a Warsaw Pact country trying to mediate between two NATO states.

IV. IDEAS OF THE FUTURE

Potentially Bulgaria seems to be less a second Hungary than a second Rumania—but without the anti-Soviet bias. Sofia's efforts at *détente* are largely limited to its own area, the Balkans. But its desire to moderate the overall East–West conflict is unmistakable. Bulgaria is interested in dissolving the pacts, although it regards bilateral alliances with the Soviet Union and with the surrounding countries as necessary or valuable. On the other hand formal ties to the northern Warsaw Pact states are seen as expendable. Sofia too wants to promote two aspects of developments in Europe and thus, like other countries, pursues two objectives—to guard against conflicts and to enlarge its own room for manœuvre. The Bulgarians interpret the principle of coexistence 'actively', like their northern and western neighbours, though this idea is only occasionally expressed.[10] All plans for arms limitations and disarmament, in the Balkans and elsewhere, would be supported by Bulgaria, in so far as this did not threaten to give rise to serious difficulties with Moscow.

For Bulgaria, the ideal situation would be if Moscow and Washington were to withdraw their fleets from the Mediterranean, and the East–West conflict disappeared from the Balkans. In a word— neutralization for South–East Europe, but with supervision and guarantees of the political *status quo* by the super-powers.

No one in Sofia believes that such a situation can be achieved

---

[9] Helmstädt, *op. cit.*, p. 55.

[10] Thus in 1966 the Bulgarian ambassador in Paris declared that relations with France had reached a stage at which coexistence had been 'superseded' and both countries had entered 'the course of active collaboration in the field of economic and cultural exchanges' (Helmstädt, *op. cit.*, p. 54).

quickly. But the vigour with which Bulgaria applies itself to this objective depends on how far the present and future leadership acquires enough strength in internal politics to apply its efforts in this direction without constant anxious side-glances towards Moscow.

CONCLUSIONS

Each of the six states linked to the Soviet Union in the Warsaw Pact is a special case in security policy. From East Berlin to Sofia there are differences in the historical background, experience during World War II, development after 1945, internal conditions and the stability of the regime. Each country has its own security problems and its own way of solving them. A similar background can lead to quite different results (like Hungary and Rumania), while different backgrounds can eventually lead to a similar policy. But despite numerous similarities and parallels, the differences are so great it is not surprising there is a lack of unity in Eastern Europe—either pro-Soviet or anti-Soviet unity. Any general statement on the security policy of Moscow's six allies, therefore, is only valid with the reservation that it *is* a generalization.

I. DANGERS

Fears of the West

All six states are relatively small countries which share one common experience (apart from the GDR which only emerged in 1949). In the past, when it came to a crisis, they were scarcely free to make their own decisions, but became objects of decision by the great powers. Today those countries lie between NATO and the Soviet Union. In so far as they have anything to fear from the West, it is from American 'imperialism' or West German 'revanchism' or both together. The rest of the NATO states only feature as a security risk because they are allied to Washington and Bonn.

Anxiety about the Americans, who during the 1950s had threatened all the Communist rulers with their programme of 'liberation', has visibly receded, but is still to be met with in some capitals and certain circles. The Vietnam war especially, but also actions like that in the Dominican Republic, have the effect of keeping such fears alive. It is true that the idea that Washington does not want a war in Europe prevails everywhere, almost without exception. But there is disagreement over whether Washington is no longer interested in expanding, or is merely deterred by Soviet nuclear strength.

Fear of the Germans can be depicted in a curve. It runs from the highest level of fear, among the SED leadership, through a deeply distrustful Poland to Czechoslovakia, where there is no longer fear, but a feeling of insecurity, drops further in Hungary where only small remnants of anxiety remain, and Rumania, where there are no fears, and then rises slightly in Bulgaria, where statements about the West German danger are given more credence. This curve gives expression to an essential distinction. The GDR, Poland, and Czechoslovakia are immediately involved in the German problem by their geographical position. But for the southern countries Germany is only a problem of security in so far as it is a European problem. However, all are agreed on one thing—there is no acute threat from the Federal Republic. But as with the United States, opinions differ about motive: whether Bonn is peaceable from inner conviction or only because forced to be so. Almost everywhere in Eastern Europe questions about the German danger meet with more hesitant, uncertain, doubtful answers when it is a matter not of the present but of the future, of some ten years hence. What gives rise to uneasiness is the inability to predict what, in the long run, this strong, alarmingly industrious-seeming West Germany will become. People would like the 'economic giant' to remain a 'political dwarf'. A guarantee is wanted that these unquiet Germans will really hold their peace. People want assurances that German nationalism will never again be given opportunities. The interest in West German domestic politics, and in relations between Bonn and East Berlin, which at times borders on interference, springs from this need for guarantees of security. From this same source comes the demand—not only from the three northern countries—for explicit recognition of the territorial and political *status quo* in Europe, as the symbol of a change of mind and intentions.

For the rest Germany, i.e. the Federal Republic and the GDR, is a matter for concern in capitals from Warsaw to Sofia, in as much as it disrupts a general European settlement. Only a few people believe that Germany will be the cause of a hot war. But a good many are afraid that the German quarrel might bring the cold war to life again.

There is no doubt about the determination of the Soviet Union to avoid a war. Since the Americans and West Germans do not or cannot want war either, fears of an East–West military conflict in Europe can largely be reduced to four points:

(1) The confrontation of two military blocs in a confined space, and the fear and suspicion with which both sides seek to preserve the balance of forces, or if possible to gain an advantage, constitute a danger in themselves.

(2) Local wars such as those in Vietnam and the Near East might involve the two world powers in a military conflict which could then reach out to Europe.

(3) Changes like those in Czechoslovakia in 1968 could lead to an East–West conflict.

(4) A similar development in East Germany, nationalist trends in West Germany, or both together, could create the danger of an explosion.

Each of these dangers is feared only by some people in some countries, and that not too acutely. Only the SED forms a certain exception here. One need not be afraid, but must take precautions—this seems to be the general attitude, given all the risks of generalization. Over the last six decades the European scene has changed so often and so fundamentally that with regard to the future caution must be one's rule. The task of giving the old world military security does not lie in preventing a war today and tomorrow, but in establishing peace so firmly that war will be impossible the day after tomorrow too.

The more the fear of war dwindles in the course of time, the greater become fears of ideological 'softening up' and economic dependence. Doubtless there is a connection here. Since the danger of war has receded, it is possible for tendencies to develop in Eastern Europe which result in greater susceptibility to liberal or national autonomy and to seduction by the West. The extent of the ideological danger differs in particular countries. Very roughly, it can be said that this fear plays a more important part in the northern countries which are more developed and closer to Europe than in the southern countries. The problem is complicated by the fact that it is judged differently within particular parties and party leaderships. The older generation is often inclined to overestimate the danger. Younger people mostly (but not always) look upon it in a more relaxed manner, and the most uninhibited and far-seeing even see in certain Western influences a useful challenge that could further the modernization of the Eastern system.

At present however there are more conservative than liberal rulers in Eastern Europe. Besides, it is the same there as everywhere—the more power and responsibility a man has, the less becomes his readiness to embark upon experiments and take risks. Finally, since Moscow judges the ideological danger to be particularly serious, this will continue to have an overriding importance.

Fears of the East

The Soviet fear of 'softening up' of their allies can be seen over the last two decades. Of the seven states that founded the Warsaw Pact with Moscow in 1955, one has left the alliance (Albania). Two countries have at one time felt acutely threatened by the Soviet Union (Poland in 1956, Rumania in 1968). Three have been struck by Soviet intervention (East Germany in 1953, Hungary in 1956, Czechoslovakia in 1968).[1] Only Bulgaria has been spared, a country with a traditional special relationship to Moscow almost a century old. Only among the Bulgarians are there to be found sympathies for their great Eastern

---

[1] There has, however, been a notable difference: in Budapest and Prague the Soviet troops fought against a liberal regime, in East Berlin they saved an orthodox one.

neighbour, or at least lack of hostility. Among the population of all the other states there are antipathies to the Soviet Union, sometimes considerable. Among the party leaderships only two have been able to avoid serious conflict with the Kremlin (East Berlin and Sofia), and both of these have paid particular regard to Moscow for special reasons.

This historical survey shows only the potential dangers, not the present position. Precisely because of these earlier conflicts Warsaw, Prague and Budapest make an effort to avoid difficulties with Moscow. All the party leaderships, perhaps with the exception of the Rumanians, feel Soviet support to be useful or even necessary—for some of them to deter threats of every kind from the West, and for all as an ultimate guarantee of their own rule. Joined to this is the natural solidarity of ruling minorities. If one falls, the rest are threatened too. On the other hand, each regime must create its own base in its country. This is in Moscow's interest also. But the ways of winning from the population tolerance, agreement or even popularity lead, after a certain point, to the danger of a conflict with Moscow. All the regimes in fact have found some kind of compromise between international duty and national inclination. Some of these compromises are relatively satisfying, some not very much so. In any case, however, it is a question of a balancing act, with the danger of a fall.

Consequences

Through all the differences in detail one thing shows clear: the main security problem for countries between the Baltic and the Black Sea is not a war between East and West, but the dangers of an ideological 'softening up' and a Soviet intervention. It is hardly the territorial *status quo* that needs protection but the political. Traditional ideas of creating security by military agreements, guarantee agreements and supervisory institutions do not—in the East European view and in fact—go to the core of the matter. They derive from the thinking of the 1950s, when the East–West conflict was so sharp that it seemed to contain a danger of war. Today security in Europe is almost exclusively a political and no longer a military question. Plans for arms limitation or reduction are not thereby made superfluous, but their realization will only become possible and have a beneficial effect if they form part of a policy geared to the real security problems.

The absence of serious anxiety about a NATO attack explains why a good deal goes by the name of security in Eastern Europe that has little to do with security but a great deal with the interests of the country in question. It can be said, with a certain exaggeration, that security in Europe means the following:

For the GDR recognition as a state;

For Poland recognition of the Oder–Neisse frontier;

For Czechoslovakia and Hungary more freedom of manœuvre in internal policy;

For Rumania more independence of Moscow;

For Bulgaria neutralization of the Balkans and the Mediterranean.

All the East European countries, when they speak of security in Europe, mean more contact with Western Europe (though this is least true for the GDR). Apart from Poland, it is hard to find anyone in Eastern Europe who gets excited over the subjects of preventing war and keeping the peace. But in almost all these countries one meets many people who reply to questions about European security with complaints over obstacles to East–West trade, and similar matters.

This evaporation of the fear of war also explains why it is impossible to find out anywhere, either publicly or privately, what the European security system everyone talks about is actually to look like. For the Soviet Union's allies this is of course partly because they carry too little weight, militarily and politically, to be able substantially to influence the planning and realization of such a system. But this is only part of the explanation. Talk of the security system remains purely rhetorical, primarily for two reasons:

(1) An arrangement acceptable to both sides seems hardly thinkable. In the military field alone it is notoriously difficult to agree upon a really balanced force reduction, because the defence structure of the two sides is different. For example, one cannot offset one tank against another when one side has a strong advantage in anti-tank weapons.

More important is the political aspect. A system protecting each against all may work on paper. In practice, however, in the event of a serious conflict, either the common interests of the Western countries and Eastern governments respectively would be automatically re-established, or the appropriate super-power would assert its claim to protect and dominate in 'its own' area. In Eastern Europe the division of the continent into two spheres, defined by ideology and power politics, corresponds too closely to what is intended or desired for it to be believed there that this situation could or should be replaced by a 'system'.

(2) A security system resting on East–West agreement promises little protection against the dangers that are really feared. Even an assurance such as, for example, Brandt has given the GDR, that it is not intended to change the Socialist order of society 'by force', though important, is of only limited value. Even the removal of certain radio stations and programmes and such-like, would only partly set at rest the anxieties of Communist politicians. Perhaps activities with no recognizable 'softening up' objective are even more dangerous, because they do not look like propaganda and have an effect simply in themselves.

A security system could give protection against Soviet intervention to a certain extent only. If the West promised strict respect for the political *status quo*, Moscow would presumably be more hesitant to use force against too independent-minded Socialists. The Kremlin would be bound to show more restraint if its intervention would upset an agreed East–West troop balance, and therefore would no longer be simply an internal bloc conflict. But the main doubt among East Europeans about the chances of putting into practice such a system is this: if it endangers the Soviet claim to dominance in the other Warsaw Pact countries, the Soviet Union will not agree to it.

II. SECURITY POLICY AND CONCEPTS OF THE FUTURE

There are in Eastern Europe two concepts of how to create security. The first is represented in its pure form by the GDR and to a certain extent by the Soviet Union, and also Poland. It rests on the assertion that the international class struggle has become more acute and that the danger from the West has therefore become greater. Security is offered only by strengthening the 'forces of peace', the Eastern camp. The objective must be to manœuvre the Americans, the main power of 'imperialism', out of Europe and to isolate the enemy of the *status quo*, the Federal Republic. This is security through confronting, or weakening, the opponent.

The second concept is represented in part by the Soviet Union and Poland, and otherwise by all the other Warsaw Pact countries. It is based on the belief that in the atomic age security cannot be created by sharpening the conflicts with the hope of victory, but only by *détente* and compromise. Thus the objective should be to moderate the conflicts and to overcome, step by step, in bilateral contacts, negotiations and agreements, obstacles that at present seem insuperable. The concurrent preservation of the East–West balance is regarded partly as desirable and partly as unavoidable. Thus the Americans are seen in some East European capitals as a necessary or useful counterweight to Soviet supremacy. Further important elements in this theory are the following:

(1) Politically speaking, 'atmosphere' is something altogether real. Thus an improvement in the East–West climate means making political progress. In Western Europe this idea often runs into scepticism. People are inclined to regard as propaganda anything not demonstrated by agreement in concrete questions. But the East European outlook is backed up by an understanding of how the source of disagreement often lies in mutual distrust. Personal contacts and the creation of trust cannot remove conflict of interest, but they are often indispensable preconditions for doing so.

(2) Even—or particularly—small countries can achieve something

through systematic small-scale work, both influencing the super-powers and also imperceptibly changing the whole situation.

(3) Possibilities of effective action in these respects arise only from time to time. Favourable circumstances regularly give way to un-favourable. So it is a question of making use of opportunities, instead of doing what the West mostly does—letting them pass by in after-thoughts, reservations and debates about principle.

Whether the Warsaw Pact's policy is guided by the first or the second concept depends largely upon which of two things seems more impor-tant to Moscow—preserving the unity of the camp or coming to an agreement with the West (thus at the same time loosening the co-hesion of NATO and making it possible for the Soviet Union and the rest of Eastern Europe to benefit from the West European economy). Of course the Kremlin tries to combine the two. It follows the prin-ciple of as much unity in the East as possible and as much collaboration with the West as necessary. Moscow's allies, on the other hand (except for East Berlin), want to reverse this order of priorities—as much unity as necessary and as much collaboration with other Europeans as possible. But since the Soviet Union decides upon the guide lines for the Eastern bloc's policy, co-operation across the East–West frontiers will progress only slowly, interrupted by set-backs (as after 21 August).

In practice this means, in the view of most East Europeans, that the dissolution of the military alliances that is constantly urged will remain propaganda, either completely or at least for the next ten or fifteen years. Nor is a complete withdrawal of foreign troops to be counted on within a foreseeable period—not only because the Soviet Union does not believe it can afford this. For its allies, however, both are still living goals and wishes. Warsaw and Prague would welcome withdrawal of Soviet troops and so probably would Budapest, but hardly East Berlin. Bucharest and Sofia too, which have no Soviet troops in their countries, would also regard a military disengagement as a great advance.

Thus abolition of the pacts is in the interest of all Moscow's allies (with the probable exception of the GDR). On the one hand it is thought that in this way the United States and the Federal Republic would be deprived of an instrument with which to exercise pressure upon the East European states. On the other hand dissolution of the pacts would deprive Moscow of the opportunity to demand political discipline in Eastern Europe for military reasons. At the same time the bilateral treaties of assistance with the Soviet Union and between the other Warsaw Pact states would continue, which is what most of the Socialist regimes wish. But to some of them, above all Warsaw and East Berlin, the network of bilateral alliances does not seem to go far enough. They regard dissolution of the pacts as acceptable only if these are replaced by comprehensive disarmament or security agreements with the West—a security system.

They cannot as yet do without Moscow's protection, but would like to escape from its domination as far as possible. A radical change of circumstances, removing both the domination and the protection of the Kremlin, is therefore not in the interest of most East European regimes. The bond with the Soviet Union gives rise to great resentment, and severe restrictions, but all the same Moscow provides a guarantee of two things:

(1) An end to all local disputes between neighbours, and the prevalence of peace in Eastern Europe.

(2) Security for the development of the as yet unstable social order of these states—most of them still young historically.

The Kremlin's allies are not yet in a position to act as truly sovereign Socialist states on the European stage, i.e. without its support. Their strength is too slight and their economy too little developed for them to avoid the danger of coming under the influence of the larger West European states. This is not a question of the existence of the states or their territorial extent. Even a democratic form of Socialism, such as the Czechs and Slovaks tried to create for themselves in 1968, would probably have had only limited prospects of escaping from the pull of the capitalist West. For Czechoslovakia, with its industrial tradition, such a development would be economically advantageous. But for most of the Warsaw Pact countries, whose industrialization is still in its beginnings, there would be a danger—in the view even of some non-Communist Europeans—of being held back in their industrialization programme. The memory of having once been an agricultural appendage to Western Europe lies deep. It is true that today all the East European economies are dependent on the Soviet Union. Thus they are acting economically within a framework that more or less corresponds to their level of development, and therefore seems to offer them further possibilities of development.

The conclusion drawn by thoughtful East Europeans is as follows: We must reach a stage, in growing collaboration with Western Europe, but independently of it, which makes it possible for us to deal with the West Europeans on an equal footing. Only when we are capable of being partners will we be accepted as such. In this view, and probably in reality too, the core of the European security problem consists in the fact that for historical reasons the Eastern part of the continent has lagged behind the Western. It is above all this under-development that causes the former to need protection. The ideological conflicts are in large part, though not only, the expression of 'super-structure', of the difference in degree of development. If the East Germans or Poles had something like the same standard of living as the West Germans or the French, they would have more freedom also, and the East–West border would diminish in importance, in people's minds and in practice. This basic conviction of most politically-minded East Europeans (and not only those who think in ideological terms) points to a development that would be prolonged but would lead eventually, in their view, to a position relatively free from danger, and politically rather satisfying—Western Europe must help Eastern Europe to stand on its own feet economically, in order that the economic and ideological danger from the West may disappear. This would not, it is true, solve these countries' second security problem, but it would greatly reduce it. The Soviet Union would not need to have so much fear that countries whose Socialist order largely satisfied the population might go over to the other camp.

Of course the East European states' most important security problem, their lack of economic and internal political consolidation, can only be removed in the course of a long process. The further this process advances, the greater become the opportunities for joint European arrangements. Only states that are stable in domestic politics can become more mobile in foreign policy. Only countries which are less afraid of Western 'softening up', and have less need of Moscow's protection for their social order, can function effectively as factors in a European order. Only regimes which, while naturally taking account of national defence, hardly have to trouble about defending their own rule, are in a position to build across the East–West border a network of bilateral links that would in practice rule out a war, and be able gradually to emancipate Europe from the domineering influence of the semi-European super-powers.

At the same time all, even the Rumanians, are clear that any progress can only be relative. Small and even medium-sized countries, like Poland, can never again be sovereign in the classical sense. In the first place because, as neighbours of a super-power, they will remain in its sphere of influence, and in the second, because a modern economy demands a large context, and restricts both economic and political room for manœuvre. For any realistic planning what is in question is not dependence, but only its extent. And the objective is to complement ties to the East with ties to the West. There is a desire to be not merely East Europeans, but Europeans.

Agreements on external security, too, will only become possible and meaningful with growing internal security. As is well known, the main difficulty in such agreements lies in the double function of Soviet armed forces within other Warsaw Pact countries. On the one hand they deter NATO. On the other, they guarantee the loyalty of the states in which they are stationed. Thus the military result of troop reduction or withdrawal has distinct political consequences. Only in so far as Moscow no longer has to make up the defects of the political balance by military means will the Soviet Union be able to enter into treaty arrangements—on zones of arms limitation and collaboration, on troop withdrawals, and on undertaking to impose collective restraints on an aggressor, whoever he may be and whomever he attacks.

The motto of Bonn's policy in the 1950s, that it was pointless to talk about East-West *détente* without removing the causes of tensions, here receives a belated justification—but in a different way from that intended in the Federal German capital at that time. It is not the division of Germany that is the main problem. Removing the causes of tension means much more evening out the difference of level between the two parts of the continent, which is not the fault of Eastern Europe. This means strengthening the East European countries without banking on political advantage, so as to make them effective partners in cooperation. This is also the basic idea behind the Budapest appeal for 'security and collaboration'—to create more security by more collaboration, and make possible more collaboration by more security. The second is already more important than the first.

The precondition for such a development, in the East European view, is that the West respects both the territorial and political *status quo*. Arms limitation, troop withdrawals and dissolution of the blocs are steps that could be initiated at a given level of collaboration, and then be accelerated. But all this would be not so much progress in itself as a formal recognition of progress already achieved in practice. Although there are here certain differences between the northern and southern states of the Warsaw Pact—because there is more belief in the north in negotiated arrangements, and in the south in the results of accomplished facts tacitly accepted—there is a large measure of agreement on one thing: the problem of security in Europe can no more be 'solved' than any of the other real problems, or at least only by force. The only thing possible is gradually to reduce it to unimportance.